Luther M. Schaeffer

Sketches of Travels in South America, Mexico and California

Luther M. Schaeffer

Sketches of Travels in South America, Mexico and California

ISBN/EAN: 9783337319632

Printed in Europe, USA, Canada, Australia, Japan

Cover: Foto ©Andreas Hilbeck / pixelio.de

More available books at **www.hansebooks.com**

SKETCHES OF TRAVELS

IN

SOUTH AMERICA,

MEXICO AND CALIFORNIA.

BY
L. M. SCHAEFFER,

NEW-YORK:
JAMES EGBERT, PRINTER, 321 PEARL STREET.
1860.

TO

MY BELOVED WIFE,

𝕮𝖍𝖎𝖘 𝕭𝖔𝖔𝖐 𝖎𝖘 𝖆𝖋𝖋𝖊𝖈𝖙𝖎𝖔𝖓𝖆𝖙𝖊𝖑𝖞

INSCRIBED.

PREFACE.

While pursuing a journey to and from California, some years since, and during my sojourn there, I kept a daily record of "what I saw and did." It was a source of great interest and pleasure to me, especially as it was written and continued at the desire of the dear and valued friend to whom this book is dedicated. And being a stranger, wandering among strangers, often deprived of all congenial society, it became my chief delight to note down my impressions of the countries I visited.

Of course, my recollections of events and occurrences are stronger and more vivid than they would otherwise have been, and since my return many questions having been asked by acquaintances relative to a miner's life &c., frequent reference to my journal has been made. One of the editors of a religious paper, who had often listened to my reminiscences of a life among the miners, solicited me to contribute articles for his paper, which appeared under the signature of Quartz: and were continued until I had communicated the principal incidents of my three years absence. These articles, it gives me pleasure to say, were favorably received, and I have been frequently requested to publish them in book form. They are now offered to the public, with diffidence and some little hesitancy—and while they may possess no literary merit, still a full and correct history of events which came under my own observation, will, it is hoped, compensate for other deficiencies.

L. M. S.

Frederick, Md., 1860.

CHAPTER I.

THE CALIFORNIA GOLD FEVER—A BERTH SECURED—LEAVING NEW YORK—SEA SICKNESS—SUN SET—CONFUSION ON BOARD THE SHIP—A SIGHT OF LAND, &C. &C.

THE excitement attending the first discovery of gold in California was intense as it was universal. Indeed it was considered as an epidemic, and those who determined to seek their fortunes in that far off land, were said to have caught the California gold fever. A voyage thither, was at that time attended with vexatious delays and annoying inconveniences; yet tempted by the almost fabulous tales of fortunes acquired as if by magic, thousands of venturesome youth and even men advanced in years, left home and friends, dared the dangers of the deep and endured the hardships of the pioneer's life to secure a portion of the glittering metal. Early in the year 1849 I first conceived the idea of a trip to California, and repaired to New York to gain all the information I could, purchase my outfit and secure a berth in one of the many sailing vessels leaving that port.

After numerous delays and disappointments, I succeeded in obtaining passage in the ship Flavius. On Saturday, March 24th, 1849, my younger brother W. and myself sat down to breakfast together for the last time; our hearts saddened by the reflection that perhaps we might never again enjoy that privilege. Although the meal was inviting, I had no disposition to eat. In vain my brother, in his efforts to conceal his own feelings, urged me to partake heartily, for I felt so *peculiarly queer!* so much like a school boy, about to leave his happy home, for a six month's residence beneath the roof of some rigid school or seminary, that I had no appetite for either food or drink. "Come, gentlemen your time is up." I bade farewell to my acquaintances about the hotel and followed my kind friends, listlessly to the wharf. It was not, that the ship Flavius was pronounced by some, unseaworthy, not that others declared she would rot ere we reached California, that I felt so sad and gloomy; oh no, but because I was about to separate from a few highly valued friends, and I dreaded the long time that must elapse ere we would meet again.

As we hove in sight of the Flavius, we saw crowds of men, women and children standing on the wharf—some were taking a last farewell, others were imparting excellent advice, which I thought was *listened to with one ear and rapidly passed out of the other*, and others again were mingling tears of love, grief and hope, for even in that hour of departure, they were anticipating the pleasure of a future meeting. But hark! man overboard—"throw over a rope"—"stand back men"—"now, pull up—hold"

—he is safe. A son of Neptune, "had a brick in his hat," and the weight being top-heavy, caused him to lose his balance, he went in drunk and was pulled out sober! Our " A, No. 1, coppered and copper-fastened" ship Flavius, was riding at anchor as cosily as a cape pigeon just after a storm. " All aboard," whew! what a rush to the ship— "Man the windlass"—the sailors sang lustily—cheers were given and returned—we were soon gracefully sailing from the wharf and forest of masts, under the "immediate assistance" of a steam-tug. Many friends of the California bound passengers were on board. The band of music engaged for the occasion struck up *Yankee Doodle*. Away we went, every passenger excited, each one gazing intently upon the vast Metropolitan city, as we receded from its piles of brick and stone.

I knew as much about a ship as a backwoodsman, and when the anchor was let go, those of us, who were unacquainted with the sudden splash of the anchor in the water, and the rattling of the heavy linked chain, started, and cried out, "what is that?" to the infinite amusement of the " old salts," who took especial delight in watching the blunders of *landsmen*. The steamer carried us to the Quarantine landing; and as she parted from us, cheer upon cheer was given and returned with a hearty will, hats and handkerchiefs were waved aloft. Good bye, and good bye was given and returned until the steamer passed out of sight—and we were left alone to await the coming of the Captain, who did not come aboard until the following day, the 25th, when we "gold hunters" saluted him with cheers and sang in right good style Hail Columbia. The pilot took command, and off we sailed with a stiff breeze, and when we were out sight of land, hemmed in by the horizon, the pilot left us, and now we felt that we were bound in earnest for California. A few passengers were sea sick for a day or two—and if any one can imagine a fellow being utterly wretched, perfectly indifferent as to whether the ship kept straight on her course or sank beneath the waters, some idea may be formed of the awful sufferings of sea-sick voyagers. Passengers rushed to the table without the slightest order or system, the strongest secured the most food, and the proceedings on board were so aggravating, that we held a meeting, drew up rules and regulations for our comfort and convenience; after which we managed to live along more comfortably.

Monday, April 30th. Beautiful weather, lovely sunset, His majesty gracefully descended below the horizon, leaving a sky richly colored, now representing a magnificent viaduct, underneath a fiery flame—and then assuming a more calm and lovely aspect, seeming as though the Heavens were transformed into a matchless panorama of meadows, lakes and rivulets, and these again swept out of sight by a gorgeous curtain of scarlet and crimson hues.

About midnight, we crossed the "equatorial line," a fact impressed upon all by the performance of that absurd and contemptible ceremony, of Neptune, demanding homage of those passengers, who had "never before crossed the line." However, I ought not to complain, for his Highness, very kindly spared me the fine and punishment Not so with some others, who not only received a "terrible ducking" of salt water—but had slush and black paint thrown over them. Our Captain, seemed to enjoy the sport heartily—but I could not relish the foolish custom as much as some others did.

Tuesday, May 15th. About 10 o'clock, A. M., we came in sight of Cape Frio—which presented a pleasing and interesting view. We had so often and so long been wishing for only a "snuff" of land, that our hearts beat high, when we strained our eyes to catch a glimpse of the distant shore. Rio de Janeiro is only about eighty miles distant. Towards evening the water assumed a light green color—we were on soundings. Owing to the rather dangerous channel, and there being no pilots at Rio, as at most other seaports, we "took in studding sails, and laid to" until morning. The sunset was attended with wondrous beauty—descending behind a lofty hill, which seemed to have just jumped from under the water, and on either side of which, chanced to be a vessel, the whole presenting a novel and lovely scene. As he disappeared the clouds assumed a rich golden hue, followed as usual by a flame colored sky, which continued until night advanced.

As we hoped to effect an anchorage ere twenty-four hours, and a heavy dew was falling, I sought my "bunk" and was soon wrapt in slumber deep and sound.

CHAPTER II.
RIO DE JANEIRO.

Wednesday, May 16th, 1849. Ship ahoy! Where are you from? But before our captain could satisfactorily answer, there came a more terrible order from the fort. Ship ahoy! Keep from shore—put out your boat—steer north! Here then, was excitement—the night was dark—we heard the loud roar of the breakers, and found we were in a cross current, almost becalmed, and drifting towards the shore of rocks. Over was tossed our long-boat: in jumped strong, stout men, and away they pulled and worked, but still was our faithful old ship drifting towards the shore, amid roaring waves and vociferous shouts from the fort; confusion reigned supreme. Some wanted the anchor let go, others were preparing for a watery grave, or a sudden hurl against the rugged, naked, slimy rocks. When, ah! all at once, we heard from the fort—all safe! all safe!

A brilliant light was displayed on the top of the wall of the fort, which was soon answered by a rocket from the city, denoting that the authorities were aware another vessel had entered their harbor. Our anchor was soon let go: each man told what he did during our *imminent* danger. Of course no one was frightened! Finally, we all settled down in the arms of Somnus, dreaming, perhaps, of the loved ones at home.

As the light of another day began to peep over the rugged, romantic hills surrounding the harbor, I too, peeped over the side of the vessel to catch a glimpse of the city. Soon the Custom-house officials boarded us, and after satisfying themselves that all was right, the captain told us to go a-shore, which privilege very many of the passengers at once accepted.

A party of twelve of us engaged a boat alongside to take us ashore. Our oarsmen were black as night, and they would rise up when they pulled their oars, and dance, and sing, and whistle for the breeze to spring up, which, however, had no effect, for it was calm as a summer's morn; however, we were at last landed, and a more filthy, sickly, trifling set of beings lounging about the wharves, I have never seen before nor since, nor desire to see again. There were two hotels convenient to the landing, one of which was conducted by a New Yorker, but the accommodations were miserable. The Emperor's chapel is near by, but will not compare with the Baltimore Exchange. In almost every street we saw soldiers, nearly all of whom were blacks, parading or lounging about. The houses are generally two stories in height, no chimneys, as the climate is not only warm, but hot. Gardens, yards and cellars are no where seen. The gutters are in the middle of the streets, which are narrow and need very much the attention of the street sweeper. The mechanics and merchants, unlike our custom, congregate together; for instance, jewellers occupy one street to themselves, so through all the other branches of trade. The ladies go abroad, only to church; but as service is held every day, they can easily manage to get out; pews are not used; each person has a cushion, on which the faithful can kneel and repeat their numerous prayers.

I visited a monastery, built in 1671. I was very politely received. There is a chapel in the building most gorgeously embellished, the floors inlaid with variegated marble, the walls with porcelain and China squares, relieved by gilt and scarlet lines. There is also in the room a large China figure of our Saviour on the cross.

The navy yard next demanded my attention; but there was nothing attractive about it. One vessel was on the stocks; but I should suppose, by the time it was finished, the wood would be pretty much decayed, for all the workmen had adopted the "take your time system."

Several fountains are distributed over the city, around which hundreds of blacks were collecting water in casks, which they carry on their heads to the various families, hydrants and pipes being unknown to the Brazilians; and these poor degraded blacks carry sacks of coffee, bales and boxes on their heads, taking the place of drays and carts; but they are short lived; about seven years finishes them entirely.

In a large open square, without shade or any protection from the sun, crowds of almost naked negro women were washing and pounding clothes, the sun pouring down hot upon their uncovered heads, and yet they appear happy!

"Where ignorance is bliss—'tis folly to be wise."

The Market houses I found large and cleanly. But the meat had the appearance of lean horse flesh. They want a Yankee butcher among them. There was an abundance of fruit and flowers, birds both alive and stuffed, and fish, but vegetables and butter were not to be had at any price. Here I saw two "birds of Paradise," quite tame, certainly the prettiest birds I have ever seen.

The museum is only open to the public on Sunday. At the entrance I observed two cages, in each were two immense boa constrictors, alive and apparently disposed for a meal. In the window above was a large, lively white eagle, and pigeons thrice larger than our own. The entire exhibition is on one floor of an ordinary building, and the curiosities were chiefly stuffed birds, minerals, coins, a mummy, and pictures. I paid most attention to the birds, for I discovered that they were chiefly from our own country.

Seeing a large crowd of persons in front of one of the numerous churches, I joined them, and discovered that they were attending the burial of a wealthy citizen. None of the family were present. All the mourners were hired, each holding a lighted candle, and standing in military array, while around the corpse, which was exposed on an elevated bier, richly gilt, the officiating priests were sprinkling holy water, and chanting Latin prayers; after which the corpse was carried by four priests, followed by the crowd, into an adjoining apartment, where it was placed in an aperture in the wall and left exposed; a few more chaunts and prayers, and we were ordered out. It appears the bodies are covered with lime, and when the flesh is destroyed, the bones are thrown into a common pit.

The prevailing religion throughout the state is Roman Catholic, and crosses are placed on the top of every public building.

I found a number of Americans doing business out here, who, of course, are visited by their countrymen whenever they arrive, and appear to be prosperously employed.

Upon the whole, Rio is not a desirable place of residence, but the surrounding country is delightful; scenery grand, and people hospitable.

Our captain notified me that the ship was ready to sail, so I jumped aboard a boat, and gave a final adieu to Brazil, and was soon treading the decks of our American vessel, with the "delightful prospect" of a "sail round the Horn," in the very worst season of the year.

CHAPTER III.

LEAVING BRAZIL—SCENES ON BOARD THE VESSEL— STORMS, &C. &C.

Thursday, May 24th, 1849. "Come men, hurry aboard." The flag is flying—the signal given—our old ship is ready to set sail. "Man the windlass" was ordered—up came the anchor—the sails were unfurled—and away we sailed —but hark! from the antiquated Fort, was sounded— "Americana, ship ahoy?"—Hello, responded our Captain—"What de pass word?"—"Margarieto" was answered—"Very good, 'tis very good"—and away we sailed, glad enough to resume our voyage to California. We espied a brig ahead, which appeared to us, to be dancing a Virginia reel on the high sea; and I suppose if any vessel had been in our wake, we would have presented the same appearance. The weather was damp, chilly and windy, but did not appear to affect the spirits of the passengers, some of whom were singing "A life on the ocean wave"—and others "I'm bound for California"—the rest sought their bunks, while the Flavius kept steadily on her course. Finally all was still, save the occasional hoarse voice of the officer on deck—and the melancholy howl of the wind, as it swept through the rigging.

Thursday, May 31st. One week just elapsed since we bid adieu to Rio—having sailed eight hundred miles during that time. Passengers found amusement in catching, with hook and line, Cape pigeons and the Albatross. The pigeons were larger than our ordinary land pigeons. They are beautiful birds, looking more like ducks than pigeons, having on their breasts a soft, pure white down, which would make an Astor house pillow blush—they are web-footed, and cannot fly from deck, unless the wind strikes them, and then they stretch their wings and gracefully sail away.

One of the Albatross measured ten feet from one tip of the wing to the other, and from the back of his head to the end of his bill twelve inches. The prettiest cape pigeon was reserved and preparatory to being stuffed, was suspended from the main top—but the wind blowing hard, soon carried the beautiful prize beyond the ruthless hand of the amateur artist.

Friday, June 22d. "Three cheers,"—our Captain tells us we are "around the Horn"—and we found he was right when he said "Some of you are making a great fuss about rounding the Horn, and I'll venture the assertion we will round the Cape without any one knowing it;" and so we did—and right merry we were at the announcement. During the severest blow, when the sea rolled mountains high—wave after wave dashing over our staunch vessel, when the raging waters looked black with rage, I stood alone in the "forward hatch," holding on to "a stancheon" —watching the fury of the storm, with mingled feelings of awe and pleasure. The "hatches" were fastened down —the sails were clewed up—we had sailed for some days under "bare poles." Our days, for about a fortnight began at 9 A. M. and ended about 2 P. M., and time hung heavy upon our hands. We found most comfort in our bunks, for we could scarcely venture on deck without receiving a fall or undergoing a salt water bath.

Sunday, June 24th. This day completed three months of our tedious voyage; and this day we encountered one of the most terrific gales, we had thus far experienced. "Old Salts" declared they had never witnessed a more furious storm—we lost our "jib and foretop mast stay sail"—and felt ourselves fortunate in escaping so well. Our vessel rolled to and fro—and pitched "fore and aft" *without respect* to persons, trunks, dishes, et cetera—the wind whistled through the rigging, as though Neptune and his whole train of worshippers were engaged in serenading us.

Wednesday, July 4th. As we had anticipated much

pleasure in celebrating the memorable Fourth on board the Flavius, but when we peeped out at early dawn, we saw our anticipations were not to be realized. The sea was rough, and the rain poured down fast and heavy. Every passenger felt keenly disappointed, for we had made arrangements to have "a good time" on the glorious natal day of American Independence. However, the American people, "know no such word as fail." The passengers assembled midships, *in the saloon*, which was in reality nothing but the steerage or between decks. The author read the Declaration of Independence, and owing to the sickness of the duly appointed orator, delivered a few reremarks, followed by about twenty others—and thus with speeches, songs and sentiment, we whiled away the day, doing our best to commemorate the glorious Fourth.

Thursday, July 12th. Magnificent sun rise. The ocean during the day was calm as a lake. The atmosphere warm and agreeable, and sky and clouds presenting a succession of rich and varied views.

Whales seen at a distance, spouting water high in the air, accompanied by a noise resembling the sound of a high pressure engine. We expected to make Valparaiso before many hours, and of course every passenger was excited with the hope of soon stepping ashore once more; for hardly any circumstance can be so delightful to a sea voyager as the prospect of soon reaching port.

CHAPTER IV.
VALPARAISO AND ITS INHABITANTS.

About 1 o'clock P. M. the anchor was let go, and our dangerous and disagreeable voyage around the inhospitable coast of Patagonia was over. Each man gazed wistfully at the wild Chilian scenry, and viewed with delight the city of Valparaiso, built upon hills and surrounded by volcanic looking eminences, heartily wishing the lazy custom house officials would come on board and permit us to go ashore.

As the light of another day dawned, bringing with it the dews and cold of a Chilian morning, I anxiously peered over the side of the vessel, fearful the rain would descend and add to the gloom of my already sombre feelings. But about 9 o'clock the glorious, ever welcome sun came forth in all its splendor, dispelling the dew and dampness, and I ventured aboard a "dug out," and for two reals (25 cents) was rowed to the landing. Here I saw some of the natives lounging about the old rickety wharves, with their fancy colored blankets thrown around them, and wearing a sharp-pointed, Chinese-looking hat, which serves both as an umbrella and sun-shade.

Valparaiso is built something in the form of a horseshoe, and extends over considerable space. The general style of building is far more pleasing than in Rio. I observed some very comfortable residences, but there are many mere "Adobes." The Custom House is in front of the landing—a one storied, dull looking building. On the right is the Merchant's Exchange and Reading Room, in which I found some old New York papers. Underneath is a large ship chandlery establishment, owned by an American. To the left is an old, almost dilapidated building, called the "Hole in the Wall," and I found it a hole indeed—in which crowds were drinking the various stimulating liquors, which make fools of all who too freely imbibe. The hotels are quite comfortable, and I found the landlord of the "Baltimore House," (where I dined,) a native of old Maryland. The "Star Hotel" opposite, is presided over by Monsieur Frenchman. Passing up Main street, I found the stores numerous—goods well arranged, but prices exorbitant. Perfumery, gaudily labelled, takes well.

Along the upper part of the street small wares were displayed on the sidewalk, and as I am about as conversant with the Spanish language as with the Chinese, the incessant gabbling of the crowd was of course unintelligible. But the manners and customs of the natives are so different from our own, that I had plenty of incidents to amuse and interest me.

Whoa! whoa!—ah, here comes a fine team, a clumsy,

pig-pen looking wagon, perched on two clumsier wheels cut out of solid wood, drawn by two miserable looking oxen, which were treading along a little behind 2.40 time. And here dashed along two mules, on one of which sat a postillion, with a spur about a foot long, digging it into the sides of the mules, which were drawing a vehicle, closely resembling one of our old-fashioned, high-top gigs, in which were seated two pretty signoritas. The ladies go abroad at all times, wearing a gay colored shawl over their heads, and are polite and social in their manners. Again I was attracted by a familiar sound—the rolling and tumbling of nine-pins. I peeped into one of the numerous bowling alleys, and saw many of my own countrymen enjoying the exercise; much more lively and agreeable they seemed than when a-board their respective vessels.

Extending my walk outside of the city, I observed a large number of donkeys and goats slowly wending their way down a tortuous path, through the irregular hills. The patient, but sleepy looking donkey, not much larger than a Newfoundland dog, was laden with fire-wood and country produce, and the long-bearded goat ready to supply the inhabitants with milk. To the Chilians these animals are invaluable. In the houses of the poor, the donkey, goat, dog, cat and chicken usurp the best places, and in all probability are allowed the best fare. Fruits are abundant, so also wild game. Liquor can be had at every store, but the natives prefer light wines, leaving brandy, whiskey and gin for the foreigners to swallow. A vast quantity of wheat is raised in Chili, and its flour, usually packed in bags of about 100 lbs., has a high reputation. Indeed, Chili offers many inducements to encourage the emigration of enterprising merchants and mechanics.

The government is republican—the religion Roman Catholic; but the inhabitants appear to care more for their temporal comforts than their spiritual interests. I fear the morals of Valparaiso are not of the highest order; yet a more social, hospitable and polite people I have never met. They are remarkably fond of music; the opera is well encouraged, but in nearly every house you hear the guitar, which seems to be the universal favorite; and dancing is participated in by almost every one. Called by an acquaintance into a house, and requested to give the company a few notes on the flute, I played several of our national airs, which were respectfully listened to; but when I struck up a polka, instantly the entire company were on their feet, dancing away as merry and happy as any set of mortals could be.

I visited the fort, located on an eminence, overlooking the harbor; but as I was preparing to rest myself after my fatiguing tramp, one of the numerous soldiers ordered me to "vamose," which I did without waiting for a second command.

As nearly all the vessels that sail around the Horn make this place their rendezvous, the shipping merchants and others do a thriving and flourishing business, and the city itself is sustained by the vast amount of shipping which at all seasons congregate here.

Our vessel being provisioned, the signal for hoisting the anchor announced, I bade adieu to Valparaiso, jumped aboard a row-boat, passed several United States and English men-of-war, sprang upon the deck of our good old ship, and joined the crowd in a real American buzza for Chili, as we were fast sailing away, and heading for San Francisco.

CHAPTER V.
SAN FRANCISCO IN 1849.

After six months' endurance of the good old ship Flavius—after an almost interminable life on the Atlantic and Pacific oceans—after a surfeit of watching the rising and setting sun, the circular horizon, the numerous fishes of the deep, and listening to the roar of the angry waters, the strike of the ship's bells, to the orders of the officers, the stories of passengers and sailors—at last, on the bright and beautiful morning of September 17th, 1849, we passed the "Golden Gate," entered the capacious and magnificent bay of San Francisco, and let go the heavy anchors, amid the vociferous cheers of one hundred delighted and grateful passengers.

Only those who have been long at sea, can appreciate the happy feelings of persons, who after a long and tedious voyage, are permitted to look out upon land, and can once more tread mother earth.

I succeeded in procuring a standing place in a row boat alongside our vessel, and was soon nearing that land whose rich mineral deposits were disturbing the entire world.

"Keep down there!" "Hold still! Wait until I can fasten my boat." "Don't you see how fast the tide is running?" "There—you can go." We jumped ashore, and I stood upon the soil of California.

So long pent up on board the ship, that when I began to walk, it seemed as though the earth was heaving to and fro, like some gigantic vessel. But this feeling soon passed off, and I pushed ahead, determined to see and hear all I possibly could in San Francisco.

People from every part of the habitable globe appeared to be congregated here. Some were hurrying off to the mines—others were bartering their clothes, their saw, plane, hatchet, &c., to raise funds to enable them to reach the auriferous districts. Others, again, were driving a brisk trade in merchandise, or were engaged in hotel keeping, and preparing habitations for the coming winter.

People had no time to stop and talk. Rents were enormous, prices exorbitant, and everybody acted as though they had but a few hours only to attend to a year's business.

With the exception of a few old stone and adobe houses, the town seemed to contain nothing but tents and boarded houses, some of which were brought from the States.

I reached the great centre of attraction—the bedlam of the town—the plaza, or public square. Here was an immense crowd. I could hear music, excited men shouting, swearing, some laughing, and others looking as woebegone as though they had lost friends, money, and even hope.

Here were assembled the sporting fraternity in full force. Let us enter the blue tent on the corner, known as the El Dorado Saloon. Around the several tables are seated gamblers surrounded by all kinds of adventurers.— The Mexican, American, Native Californian, English, Dutch, French, Irish, &c. &c., clad in varied habiliments, from the glossy broadcloth to the well-worn linsey, every one watching with painful interest the progress of the game. Piles of doubloons and eagles, pistols, &c. are displayed on the tops of the tables—now a card is thrown out—down go the bets—another and another, until the fourth is thrown out. The gambler taps—the betting ceases, and the result is known. The banker raking off the largest share. A little bell is sounded. "Here, Bob! Gentlemen, what will you drink? Smoke a cigar?" Plied with stimulants, the game is renewed, and hour after hour the play is continued. There stands a pretty looking woman with dice in her hand. "Walk up gentlemen and try your luck"—and there behind a table stands a man, rolling little balls. Listen—"Come, gentlemen, here's the spot to raise your funds—walk up." Look on the wall, or rather muslin partitions—see those flash pictures—on that high box sit several musicians, whose lively music add enchantment to the scene. More rum, more excitement—some few exultant, while the losers go off one by one, looking most disconsolate, and cursing their fate.— Ah! why yield ye to temptation—why did you not obey the instruction of a good mother, or the wise counsel of a pious father. Perhaps you now remember the parting admonition of a fond wife or sister. But we have little time to moralize,—as we pass through the many elegantly furnished saloons that surround the Plaza, we find the same excitement, the same noise, bustle and confusion.

Clink! clink! clink! "Hammer away men—hurry up the building—time is money out here—the work must be done this week." So throughout the city; every body in a hurry—they walk in a hurry, and talk and eat in a hurry.

Bang! What is that? Here comes the steamer Oregon. Let us go down to the wharf and see if among her hundreds of passengers we can recognize one familiar face—no, not one—we are alone, as it were, among thousands.

But now for our letters—some consolation in hearing from friends at home. But hear! What is that you say? The steamer brought no mail!

Bah! what a disappointment to the anxious expectant.

I ascended one of the highest eminences around San Francisco, known as Clark's Point, and I could look far out upon the deep blue sea. I could see here and there a sail "beating in." In another direction I could see many sloops and schooners sailing across the bay, loaded with passengers bound for the mines.

There are two beautiful, almost circular islands in the bay, one of which is supposed to contain immense deposits of Guano. Below lay the city, and its fine harbor, containing already a vast amount of shipping, and back of it a range of hills and mountains. The day was closing, and chilled by the cold night winds peculiar to the climate, I descended, and again mingled with the crowd.— But my time for sight seeing was expended. I had to prepare for another trip, and leave this city replete with the elements of future greatness and prosperity, with good and bad men, thorough-going men, who deserved success for their enterprise, perseverance and self-denial, and be off for the mines. I bade farewell to the good old ship that carried me safely to port amid furious storms and raging seas—the old ship that held firm during the severe storms that beat hard against her—the staunch old vessel that acquitted herself so handsomely, (as the sailors express it,) and being among entire strangers—men from different parts of the States, of various characters and dispositions—I could not but feel sad as I looked upon her for the last time.

CHAPTER VI.
OFF FOR THE MINES.

"Jump aboard, men! Don't you see that black cloud rising there? Hurry up—we must cross the bay before the storm overtakes us." We hurried aboard, hoisted the anchor, and away our little schooner cut through the water "like a thing of life." But the storm overtook us, and the wind blew hard, tossing our little schooner up and down the angry waves. She rocked to and fro, was pitched upon her starboard side, and she cracked and strained as though she would break into a thousand pieces. But we weathered the storm safely, and soon lost sight of San Francisco. We were bound for Stockton, on our way to the southern mines. Our party consisted of fourteen men, each of whom, myself excepted, were accustomed to manual labor, and they feared that I could not endure the exposure, and lacked the physical strength necessary for a "miner;" but it proved in the end that the "battle is not always to the strong, nor the race to the swift."

About 8 A. M. we lay to; towards daylight a breeze springing up, we up anchor and sailed onward.

We passed Benecia, a most lovely location for a town. The numerous and abrupt hills back of the village, gave a pleasing charm to the view, all of which, as far as the eye could reach, were covered with wild oats and barley. There were several United States men-of-war and merchant ships riding at anchor, and it was thought this would become a naval station.

As we sailed on we saw two shanties on the shore, which I was told constituted the city of "New York on the Pacific."

At length we entered the mouth of San Joaquin river, a stream so narrow that I could toss from the vessel a pebble on either shore, and so shallow that not only our little craft, but others we passed, were occasionally aground, and had to wait until the tide floated us off.

Another night on board, but no sleep for any of the passengers. The myriads of musquitoes that infest the Tule, a plant growing luxuriantly in the marshes along the river, seemed to have all assembled on board our vessel; and as they were exceedingly affectionate, I could hear the passengers continually battling with their musical friends, and I longed for the light of another day. Morning came, but the heat was so oppressive, that my condition was not much improved.

I noticed large numbers of ducks, grouse, cranes, &c., flying about, and many of the passengers wished they had guns at hand, and I even, thought if one of the feathery flock would alight, and let me place the muzzle of the gun within a foot of it, I could pop it over too.

We passed the "lone tree," appropriately so called, for I could see no other tree within a long distance of it.— The ground about here seemed fit for pasturage, and doubtless by this time, through the indomitable energy of the American settlers, yields abundant harvests. The natives are too indolent and trifling to dig a foot of ground.

During the afternoon we espied Stockton, but the wind had almost died away, so we made but slow progress, and we tacked, pulled ropes, pitched canvass, and fussed about as though we were on board some large clipper. Every skipper or captain that I ever knew seemed proud of his vessel, no matter what the size or proportions.

We finally reached our landing place, and lost no time in getting out our baggage and deserting the little vessel. The town consisted of a few adobe houses and tents; in each of which liquor was dispensed and card playing going on. I observed a few miserable specimens of the native Indians loitering about, and as Stockton was the starting point for all travelers to the mines, there were many adventurers collected together, and each man would anxiously inquire for the best location to visit, the distance, route, &c. &c. There were no distinctions in society; dress did not indicate wealth or poverty. The most filthy and ragged looking "ombre" might have the biggest pile.

Now commences the first lesson as a "California miner." Poles were cut for the tent to be pitched, then firewood was brought, and then for our first meal, cooked by ourselves—let me see, what had we? Coffee as black as charcoal, pork as salt and fat as could possibly be, bread a little lighter than lead; but it was palatable and relished by all of us. The supper over, I stretched my blanket on the dusty ground, sought sleep and found it.

Another day came round, and we prepared for our tramp to the mines. We engaged a team to carry our baggage to the auriferous districts, distant about seventy miles, for which we agreed to pay the "moderate sum" of fifteen cents per pound.

About noon we struck our tent and made ready to travel towards the mines, on my favorite animal, shank's mare!

Away we went. Whew! wasn't it hot. The road dusty, scarcely any shade, and what trees we saw always happened to be out of our path.

So long pent up on board the ship, my feet were almost too tender for the journey, and when we halted for the night,

2*

I was, like the others, glad enough to throw my blankets on the cold ground, and seek rest and sleep, which was delicious to me.

About 2 o'clock we awoke, partook of "a hasty cup of tea," and marched forward, intending to rest during the day. The very ground was cracked open, the weeds were shriveled up, and the numerous toads and serpents we passed seemed the color of the earth, for this was the dry season, and dry enough it was.

On we traveled, panting, sweating and grumbling, and almost worn out, till at last we reached a beautiful stream called Stanislaus river, into which we plunged "sans ceremonie," and crossed to the opposite shore, when we quickly divested ourselves of our dirty and wet clothing, and plunged into the welcome river, fairly kissing with joy the pure and cooling waters as they gently flowed by us.

We halted on its bank for the night, the dust at least two feet deep. At early dawn we again gathered up our blankets and traveled on. Occasionally we would stop and gaze at the beautiful and picturesque scenery surrounding us.

Towards noon we came within sight of our stopping place. I could hear the rattle of the many washing machines; I could see the men digging, hauling and washing the dust containing the precious metal, and no one appeared idle. Dig, dig, pick, pick, shovel, shovel, was the order of the day, and I wondered how I could stand the hard, incessant labor necessary to achieve success.

I kept on and noticed the many tents stretched along the banks of the Tuolumne river, and I sat down upon a rock, shaded by a sycamore, to rest myself from my tedious journey. Sleep seized me, and when I awoke, the miners had quit work for the day. The noise had ceased, and I felt indeed "like one who treads alone some banquet hall deserted."

I sought the tent, under which I expected to repose for the night; but the arrangements were not completed, so with others of the party, I stretched my blankets on the ground, myself upon them, and slept soundly until morning, when we arranged our tent and sallied out in search of some suitable spot to commence mining operations, and the peculiarities and hardships of a miner's life I will describe in the next chapter.

CHAPTER VII.
LIFE AT THE MINES—WINTER OF 1849.

Hawkins' Bar, afterwards dignified by the appellation of Hawkinsville, was beautifully situated on the Tuolumne river, a narrow stream which gently flowed along, its course about as straight as a Virginia fence. Hawkinsville contained a population of about one thousand men;

not a single woman or child within fifty miles of the place.
The hardy miners "dwelt not in marble halls," but under
the fragile covering of 10 cent muslin. Preachers, doctors, lawyers, mechanics and laboring-men cooked their
provisions, mended and washed their clothing; and not
unfrequently a man who had been classically educated, and
perhaps had been professor of belles lettres in some college, might have been seen turning his "slap jacks" dexterously in the frying pan, or sitting on an old stump mending his breeches. All the citizens were on an equality;
and not unlikely, the boisterous sailor was the most successful miner.

After the day's work was over, some would engage in
reading the Scriptures, singing hymns, and talking of their
homes and future prospects; whilst others, less considerate, would gamble, get drunk, carouse and make night
hideous by their screams and incessant firing of guns
and pistols.

Our party were always up and preparing breakfast before the stars had disappeared, and would sit around the
camp-fire, smoking pipes, awaiting the dawn of day. And
what a life to lead! what hardships, exposures and self-denials men undergo for the sake of money. We were not
very successful in our mining operations, and when reports reached us that blacksmiths were wanted at Stockton at $16 per day, those of our party who were smiths,

evinced a disposition to accept the offer, and leave the mines, which were not remunerative. The smoke of discontent soon burst into a flame; a division of property was demanded, and our "Mutual Beneficial Association," which was to continue at least six months, was, like all California parties, numbered among "the things that were." I soon found that "might makes right," and I was told to vacate the tent and its conveniencies at once. Too glad to escape from men so uncongenial and selfish, I made no complaint; like the studious owl, I said nothing, but kept up a deal of thinking.

A neighbor offered me the use of his tent and board at nine dollars per week, which I accepted, and soon had my bed and et ceteras transferred to his establishment, the bill of fare to consist of salt pork of questionable age, musty crackers and tip top coffee, provided some body knew how to make it. However, I relished the food and never enjoyed better health. The climate is so pure that, exposed as I was, to all kinds of weather, hard work, and no proper shelter or conveniences, I could not in any other part of America have enjoyed better health.

With only a knife, broken pick and pan, did I, day after day, search for the glittering metal, secreted amid rocks, crevices and dirt. The general custom was to dig down until a stratum of earth was reached, which indicated the presence of gold. The earth was then shoveled into the box on top the rocker, water was constantly poured upon it, whilst the rocker was shaken to and fro; at night that left in the bottom of the cradle was carefully scooped up, and washed in a pan, and the profits of the day's labor soon known.

Some of the miners conceived the idea that the bed of the river contained the richest deposits of gold. A company was formed, a canal dug, a dam constructed, and the water was to be turned from its natural channel. Now were the men excited, and with three cheers the water was turned into the canal, and every one anxiously waited the time to examine the bed of the river, which had been undisturbed, peradventure, for ages. The order to begin work was announced the next morning, and the one hundred men, comprising the "Tuolumne River Mining Company," began to dig up rocks and mud, and the rattle, rattle, of the many cradles, resounded through the adjacent forests, causing the untutored Indian to look with affright at the busy scene before him. The result of the day's labor yielded to the Company the most gratifying evidence of success, and each man, as he threw himself upon his blanket to rest from the arduous labors of the day, could scarcely sleep, so excited was his mind, hoping that in a few weeks he could return to his friends in the States well rewarded for his enterprise, &c.

But "This world is all a fleeting show, For man's illusion

given," for next day the rain poured down incessantly, the river rose rapidly, and by night the artificial dam was washed adrift, and the hard labor of weeks was destroyed in a few hours. But men who had become accustomed to disappointment and mishaps were not the persons to despair—no such words as "give up" to be found in their vocabulary. When the storm ceased they recommenced the construction of the dam, and their ultimate success emboldened others at the various mining districts to, not only turn the course of rivers, but to dig down hills, banks, and accomplish almost incredible feats of labor, using only pick, shovel and hammer for their tools. Solicited by an acquaintance, who was working a profitable claim, to assist him in getting out "dirt," prior to the filling up the claim with water, (the season of rain and storms had now set in,) I consented, and early next morning was busy digging in a hole at least twenty feet deep.

From unmistakable indications, I inferred, this was not the safest place, for as the rain poured down loosening the earth, I feared the banks would cave in. I noticed also a large stone projecting at the top of the bank, and expressed myself unwilling to work much longer : however, I continued the day out, and was glad to rest my bruised and aching limbs at night. In the morning I was at my post again, but emphatically informed my friend, Mr. S—d, of Georgia, that I could not in justice to myself and those

I had left at home, risk my life under such threatening circumstances. Mr. S—d changed my work, remarking at the same time that he had left a wife and six children in Georgia, that he valued his life, and the happiness and peace of his family as much as I did or could; and that I was totally unacquainted with such work; that he had more experience, and knew there was no danger. But alas! how often are men mistaken! How little they know what an hour may bring forth!

My duty was now to carry stones and dirt in a bag, on my shoulder to the rockers, about twenty yards distant, and the first step I took, I slipped, and my foot pressed clear through my shoe. On I kept, and when I was about to tumble the load down, I hardly remember which fell first, the bag or myself, and a more mud-bespattered individual is rarely to be seen. Of course, my fall and appearance caused the crowd to shout with laughter.

The next load I succeeded in getting down more easily, (because it was lighter,) but as I was about to return, some one called out hastily, "Here, here, doctor, doctor, come quick; the bank has caved in, burying poor Sherwood—run!" We all started off and found, just as I had predicted, the bank caved in, poor Sherwood covered up entirely, and Dr. P——, of New York buried to the waist. We pulled the doctor out, who, although much bruised, was not seriously hurt, and we then rapidly and cautiously sought for Sherwood. The crowd assembled around were painfully excited; not a word was spoken. We all feared the worst, but still hoped. At last I espied the hat of the unfortunate man; and I saw the brains scattered around, and discovered that the very stone he was warned to look out for, had killed him! We raised the cold and inanimate body, and slowly and sadly carried it to the tent, which he had left but a short time previous in good health, good humor and happy anticipations.

The grave was dug on a hill near by, shaded by a wide-spreading oak, and those of us who knew him best and worked with him, followed his lifeless remains to the grave as mourners. The beautiful and impressive burial service of the Episcopal church was read, and we departed for our homes, filled with sadness and melancholy at the untimely fate of one who was suddenly hurled into eternity, far from his family, his home and his kindred. Requiescat in pace.

My landlord informed me that, in consequence of the high price and scarcity of provisions, and the impossibility of receiving supplies, on account of the wretched condition of the roads, " he could not board me any longer." This was bad news for me, and the only *hotel* in the place could offer me no relief, for their boarders *took their meals in the open air*, and slept wherever they could. I concluded to hitch up my reliable shanks' mare and start for San Francisco. Meeting an acquaintance who was also anxious to leave, we soon disposed of every article we did not absolutely require, and prepared to start in a couple of days. I could leave this place without any regrets, for I left no one to mourn after, and I knew of no particular spot to cause me to regret parting from. Not so in other portions of California, of which I will speak hereafter.

CHAPTER VIII.

LEAVING THE MINES.

On Tuesday, November 20th, 1849, two acquaintances and myself, strapped our bedding and clothing on our backs, and bade farewell to Hawkinsville. We slowly ascended the rough hill, which sheltered from the piercing winds the little village of tents, and pushed forward for Stockton in good humor with ourselves and the " rest of mankind."

The roads were in a miserable condition, and occasionally we halted to scrape off the putty like mud which impeded our progress.

I had purchased before starting, two pounds of crackers, at seventy-five cents per pound, and when we came across a beautiful rivulet, we sat down to feast upon our meagre fare, but would have enjoyed something more substantial. On we pressed, scaling mountains, crossing valleys and creeks, then ascending high hills, almost exhausted, until at last we came in sight of the " Mountain House," at which place we proposed to spend the night. The "Mountain House" was simply a large tent; and the bull dog-visaged landlord, notified the many travelers who had met there, that supper would be ready soon, and all who partook and paid for it, were entitled to spread their blankets under the tent—of course. We all agreed, and about 8 o'clock, supper was announced, which consisted of half baked bread, salt beef, salt fish, and something called coffee—for which each paid two dollars. We spread our blankets on the ground, and expected to have a comfortable night's rest; but the rain descended fast and heavy, and we had to shift about to protect ourselves from the storm.

Early in the morning, most of us bound downward, agreed to proceed, although it was raining hard. We had a miserable time of it, the roads were muddy and almost impassable. Our packs saturated with water, were twice as heavy as when we started. Sometimes we would overtake others in the road ; then again get separated, and I felt indifferent as to which road I took, or whither it would lead me. Finally we reached "Knight's Ferry," I tumbled into a boat, was ferried across, and made rapid tracks for a large tent a short distance ahead, threw my bundle down and rested. Here were collected together a large number of men, some bound to the mines, and others on their way to Stockton.

Among the party was a handsome youth, son of a well known auctioneer of Baltimore; a fortnight afterwards I met him in San Francisco, and learned in conversation, that he had contracted a cold on this trip. Poor fellow! One week later he was numbered with those who have gone to "that bourne from whence no traveler returns."

The proprietor of "Knight Ferry House" proved to be a kind-hearted man, and his polite attention to my wants will never be forgotten by me. For, oh, how delightful to a wayworn traveler to meet with even one person that exhibits a little of the milk of human kindness.

I breakfasted on fresh deer steaks, fresh mountain trout, hot rolls and excellent coffee, for which I paid $1 50. I observed a number of Indians loitering about, and was informed, that from them mine host procured his deer and trout

The night was very inclement, and my considerate landlord, observing my wearied appearance, kindly furnished me a piece of oil cloth on which to spread my blankets. There were about fifty men lying under the tent, and as each one was tired out, it was not long before sleep quieted the motley crowd; about midnight I awoke and discovered somebody using my feet for a pillow; I politely requested whoever it was, to look out for some other rest-

ing place, as I was too much fatigued to allow any one
to rest on me. No answer being returned, I had no alternative but to kick off the intruder, no matter what the
consequence; so jerking my feet from under the interloper, I brought him a pretty severe blow on the head,
when up sprang a large dog, howling and leaping from
one person to another, producing a violent commotion in
the camp. Every one cried out, "Who disturbed that
dog?" "Who made that fuss?" Poor brute, he continued howling and jumping around, getting more frightened every moment—boots and whatever could be reached, were thrown at him, until at last he sprang
through the canvas to the great relief of the lodgers.
Of course, during the excitement, I was as still as a mouse,
and like Daniel O'Connell's attorney at a private party,
who, when asked to make a speech, arose and said—"Gentlemen, mum's the word!" After this little episode, which
was not set down in the programme we all slept comfortably until morning, which, fortunately for us, was
bright and clear, and after partaking of another excellent
meal, we bade our host farewell. Three of us left the ferry
together, entire strangers to each other: those with whom
I left the mines, agreed to rest awhile and follow along
at their leisure. The roads were now in a most deplorable condition, it seemed as though every time I put my
foot down, it sank out of sight; of course, we made but

slow progress. Ravines that we had passed on our way to the mines, then dry and solid, were now swift running streams, which had to be waded waist deep. Towards night, I felt my strength well nigh exhausted. I was told we would find a stopping place a couple of miles further on, but I feared I could not reach it; just then we came to a stream, rushing madly along, and some wondered how we could ford it; but I did not pause to consider about it a moment, but pressed on; the rest followed, and we succeeded in gaining the opposite shore. I felt refreshed for a time; my clothes, boots, &c., were completely saturated with water, but I soon began to weary, until at last I fell to the ground, completely exhausted. I do not know how long I should have lain there, had not some one staggered up to me, almost overcome himself, and shouted out, "Doctor, look up, don't you see that light ahead; get up, and we can reach it." I arose, and both of us stumbled on. We thought it must be some ignis fatuus, for now we could see it, again it disappeared, until at last we heard shouts of laughter. We took courage and soon reached "Red's Tent." Here was a lively party; the whole of whom had been stimulating, and with their dancing, shouting and hurraing, aroused even the well nigh exhausted travelers. I found "Red," as he was called, a clever hearted fellow, and at once asked him the privilege of making my bed under his tent; but he informed

me that those who preceded me, had *pre-emption* right.
I warmed myself and dried my wet clothes before a blazing fire in the open air, and partook of an excellent supper; charge two dollars, and with two or three others threw my blanket on the damp ground, and although the wind was high, and the night cold, I slept comfortably, and arose in the morning " as fresh as a lark."

I started off for Stockton in company with a former wholesale dry goods merchant of New York, and a son of a Georgia planter, and a pretty looking trio we were. Our clothes patched and well worn, our beds et cetera on our backs, we must have presented a ludicrous sight. We intended to breakfast further on the road, and away we tramped. Occasionally we crossed rapid streams on a log, some one had thrown over, and if we had made a misstep, there is no telling where we would have brought up. However, we got along safely, and reached the blue tent, known as the "Texas House." Here we ordered breakfast. The host was a clever old man, who, upon seeing me, exclaimed, "My dear sir, you are looking much jaded, had you not better rest here a day?" But I told him I was bound for San Francisco, and wished my journey over as soon as possible. He asked us to wait until he could cook our meal, and regretted that his larder contained so little just then. The blue tent was of so small capacity, that we preferred lying down on the grass outside, and were glad of the opportunity to rest.

Our meal consisted of coffee, bread and fried beans; and when we came from the table, not a drop of coffee, not a slice of bread, not a bean was left. I thought "mine host" certainly told the truth, when he said his larder was nearly empty. We bade the old gentleman good-bye, and plodded on; in about an hour or two, we were all tumbling in the road, suffering intense pain, occasioned, doubtless, by the half baked beans. We met a man, of whom we inquired the distance to the next stopping place. He assured us that we had but little further to travel, before we would find ' Dancing Bill's Tavern." We hurried on, still suffering from sickness, and at last espied an old log cabin, which we supposed was the place we were in search of. As soon as we entered the cabin, we called for brandy, and drank it down; but although it proved to be common Jamaica rum, we were satisfied, for it relieved us of our sickness. Not liking appearances about this place, we pushed on, hoping to make Stockton before night; but about two miles from it, one of the party gave out, and we agreed to remain with him. We gathered fire-wood, kindled a fire, and after resting a while, began to feel a disposition for supper; we had no alternative but to roast the acorns we found on the ground, and drink for our tea, water that had, fortunately for us, lodged in a mud hole! We spread our blankets on the ground, and when morning came, we thought it had been snowing during the night, so completely was the ground covered with hoar-frost. We bundled up our bedding and pushed on for Stockton, which place we reached about 9 o'clock. The town had much improved during the short time we had been absent; but as we were anxious to have this trip over, we only stopped for breakfast, and hurried down to the wharf, engaged passage on an old schooner for San Francisco, and after a tedious and disagreeable passage, reached the metropolis of California on the evening of November 28th, 1849.

CHAPTER IX.
SAN FRANCISCO.

When I stepped ashore from the old schooner which brought me from Stockton, I was surprised to observe the vast improvements that had been made during my brief absence. The "blue tent on the corner," which I described in a former letter, was displaced by a commodious two-story edifice; alongside was the "Parker Saloon" of still more elegant style and finish, and so throughout the entire square, changes had been made.

The post-office was located on a hill, overlooking the greater portion of the town and bay; and here were hundreds going and returning, anxiously inquiring for letters from home; and I, too, stepped up to the window, and inquired of the clerk if there was a letter for me. He looked, but turned coldly around and said, no! Not a solitary acquaintance had I, among the thousands moving about the city; and if any of my readers have been in foreign lands without a friend to converse with, they can imagine my feelings, when wandering amid a vast crowd, and not recognizing a single acquaintance. My clothes were stored on board a vessel lying in the stream; those I had on were not only well worn, but, like Joseph's coat, of varied colors. But as I had not yet secured a permanent lodging-house, and was not engaged in any business, I did not care how I looked, or what kind of a figure I presented, for in truth, I was not singular in this respect.

The streets were not yet planked or paved, and as the rain poured down nearly all day, they were almost impassable; but storekeepers, having an eye to business, prudently placed boxes in front of their property, which served as acceptable sidewalks for the numerous pedestrians. The gambling saloons were always crowded ; and any one could go in and view the beautiful paintings, listen to inspiring music—gamble or not gamble—drink or not drink, just as he pleased. But oh! could those gilded walls speak, what tales of sorrow, misery and wretchedness they could unfold.

The general state of society was loose; there were no refined women to throw a moral influence around the heterogeneous mass of human beings that were congregated from every part of the world. Many of the citizens had not yet fixed upon any permanent location or employment, but stern necessity compelled every one to be on the look out for something to do. I myself began to weary at the strange and busy scenes being enacted every day, and wished the season of rain and storms would end, so that I could again travel to the mines, and keep myself employed, whether I should find the "philosopher's stone" or not.

The old City Hotel, whose long, old-fashioned balcony sheltered many a citizen during the violent rain storms, was also a favorite place of resort. Here I would occasionally partake of a cup of coffee, and here I fortunately met an acquaintance, with whom I had traveled to California. From him I learned that one of my best friends was comfortably located on California street, and I lost no time in searching him out. We had a jovial meeting; we talked over our trials and hardships, and as my friend was conducting an extensive boarding-house, I at once engaged board, and soon began to feel more comfortable than

I had done for a long while. My first business was to hire a boat and bring ashore my trunk, in which I had my principal wardrobe. There being no porters at that time, I was compelled, in accordance with the fashion of the day, to shoulder my trunk and carry it about a mile to my boarding-house, not without, however, amusing the crowd along the way with several tumbles in the mud, as the burden was almost too much for my physical strength.

After a while I, too, began to speculate, and my success enabled me to live much more comfortably than I had anticipated. I was known as a doctor, collector, agent and messenger; made mattresses out of common muslin and stuffed them with shavings, peddled cigars, patent medicines and notions; and what was thought an accomplishment at home, now became the source of my greatest pecuniary profit—I mean performing on the flute.

The officials of the city government still adhered to the old Mexican titles; for instance, the City Council was known as the Ayuntamiento, the Mayor as the Alcalde, and Superintendent of Police as Prefect. But the authorities were at constant warfare with each other, and woe to the man who had dealings with judge, lawyer or juror.

On Monday, December 24th, the cry of fire was sounded. The citizens were, of course, alarmed. The houses were constructed chiefly of boards and lined with muslin.

There were no engines at that time, and no wonder every one ran, dreading the result, for the black smoke was rising up, and we saw that the beautiful " Parker Saloon" was on fire. The vast quantity of liquor in the building added to the flames. The El Dorado took fire, and for a while the black clouds of smoke, issuing from the building, hid from view the entire block; but soon the lurid flames burst forth, threatening a vast destruction of property, until determined men blew up the adjoining house, and happily prevented the fire extending further, and it had not been wholly extinguished before parties were contracting for the erection of other houses.

Tuesday, Jan. 1st, 1850. Now the rain began to pour down, and almost every day until spring, we had rain, rain, rain. Some of the streets were filled to the depth of two feet with liquid mud, many a tumble had the pedestrians into the filthy slush, and it was now my turn to laugh.

I was standing at Friend K—'s office door, in Montgomery street, one morning, when I heard a sound as of many hammers and the rattling of chains coming near me. I turned, and there came along the oddest procession I had ever beheld. It was a chain gang!—about thirty men, white and black, two by two, each chained to the other, and each carrying a heavy iron ball on his arm.— Away they went, clank, clink, clank. I followed after them, and found that the criminals marched to Clark's Point, where they were made to dig down the rugged hills, and I could not but think the system of compelling criminals to work for their *board and lodging* most excellent and productive of much good, as the public exposure would of itself deter others from committing crime.

Things were enormously high; long boots, so indispensable for walking or rather wading the streets, could not be procured for fifty dollars; stoves were scarce, and brought from one to three hundred dollars each; and board and lodging was from fifteen to thirty-five dollars per week. This was the period in the history of San Francisco which developed whatever energies a man had. Men of the finest intellectual acquirements were glad to accept of any employment that offered. I have known gentlemen, who had been accustomed not only to the comforts, but to the luxuries of life at home, occupied in carrying lumber from ship to shore, and doing various drudgery, with not half so much grumbling as those who had been used to manual labor. And why? Because the intellect predominated.—Men of correct education could sustain themselves with more ease and comfort, through all their deprivations, through all their hardships and misfortunes, than men of small mental calibre. Politeness accomplished a vast deal. Most persons would prefer dealing with men of polished manners.

I formed agreeable associations with numerous accomplished gentlemen, but my peculiar life in California often threw me among others, of manners so uncouth and boorish, that "their room was far more agreeable than their company."

Whenever a steamer arrived from the Atlantic states, crowds would flock around the post office, and it was so difficult to obtain access to the clerk, that it was finally agreed upon, that the people should fall in line, and take their turn. I have waited in this way two hours before I could succeed in getting to the window.

Another peculiarity of San Francisco life, (I am sorry to relate it,) was the total disregard of the Sabbath.— Whilst I was listening to a reverend gentleman holding forth on the Plaza, I could hear the sound of the saw and hammer, and the jingle of the money and glasses in the adjacent saloons.

A dangerous population was now coming in. Many of the escaped convicts from Sidney and from our own land, the different fighting and sporting men, were arriving. But as yet there were no outbreaks. Good citizens began to feel uncomfortable. Men armed themselves, and watched closely their property. Society was indeed of a mixed order.

The central wharf was a great point of attraction.— Here the principal steamers and sailing vessels let go their anchors; and although the construction of the wharf cost an immense sum of money, still the wharf charges were so high that the company were getting a handsome return for their outlay. You could not pass through the gate with even a small bundle without paying twenty-five cents for the privilege. Along the road to "Happy Valley"—happy only in name—were high hills of sand. A temporary railway was built, upon which rough cars were placed—these hills were leveled, the sand conveyed to the shore—and thus the bay to a considerable extent, filled up.

The changes that were going on, the improvements contemplated and in progress, were like some Oriental tale of enchantment. But the American settlers were so persevering, enterprising and thorough-going, that no wonder the indolent and inefficient native stood back, looking with unutterable surprise at the scenes enacted before him.

I walked out to the "Mission Dolores" with a friend, distant three miles from the city, then a miserable dull and filthy place, but at this time a favorite resort. The houses were constructed of mud, which soon dries hard in the sun—no windows, no glass, merely a hole in the wall; no floors, and apparently as much a shelter for dogs, cats and goats, as for the thriftless native. I noticed an old church, built of stone something like two centuries ago, which was still used by the Roman Catholic population as a house of worship. "Fandangoes" were held principally on Sabbath evenings, and if there were any pious and devout people among them, I certainly did not meet with them.

CHAPTER X.

SPRING OF 1850—MEN, MANNERS AND THINGS ABOUT SAN FRANCISCO—OFF FOR THE NORTHERN MINES—INCIDENTS OF THE JOURNEY.

The weather during the winter season in San Francisco was never intensely cold. The frequent rains occasioned a dampness and chilliness which was of course unpleasant, but when the sun came forth and dispelled the murky clouds, the temperature was invariably delightful even in mid winter;—during the summer months, no matter how hot and uncomfortable the days may have been, the evenings and nights were always pleasant—attributable to the cool and refreshing sea breezes.

My friend W——, of New York, was an excellent representative of the shrewd, go-ahead, enterprising and speculating Yankee. Landing in California with very little of the "ready cash," not knowing (nor caring to know) any person—he commenced the sale of pies and cakes—then introduced coffee and substantials; from this, although making money fast, he transferred himself to the "North River House," where he not only conducted the hotel successfully, but also in the basement, a "universal Yankee notion store," and kept several hands employed in painting houses and signs, besides having several other "irons in the fire." Many of the Flavius' passengers, residing in San Francisco, generally met here, and my leisure time was very pleasantly occupied. There was one passenger we rarely saw or heard of, who had left at home a wife and several children; a man who had, undoubtedly, been well educated, of fine conversational powers, and who delighted in speaking of his wife and little ones. But, alas! the uncontrollable thirst for liquor soon removed him from this transitory life. He had pitched his tent in one of the vilest localities of the town, and passed his brief life among men whose very breath was so surcharged with liquor, that I should have hesitated to place a candle near them.

I was solicited to administer upon his estate, but declined in favor of an older and more experienced friend; I consented however, to take an inventory of his effects, and found it an exceedingly distressing office—distressing to look upon the cold and inanimate corpse, and think of the family at home, of the little children now bereaved of a father; it was sad to gaze upon the portraits of the different members of his family; sad to think, he died in a strange land, without the consoling companionship of those he so often talked about; and sadder yet, that he, who was possessed of fine business capacities and many excellent qualities, whose opportunities for success in life and for contributing to the happiness of others, were so numerous, should thus pass away—his only enemy—himself. A few of us, who had traveled with him to California, made arrangements for the proper disposition of the body, and on a Sunday afternoon, the sky above clear and beautiful—the air mild and balmy—everything in nature so lovely, as to make one feel glad that a kind Providence had permitted us to continue in health and strength, and thus far to resist temptation, we accompanied his mortal remains to the then only Protestant church, (Episcopal) of which the deceased had been a member, and after the reading of the usual burial services, we carried the body to a wagon, and sadly followed to the burial ground, the last remains of poor ——.

Another of my fellow passengers was one of those erratic geniuses who lacked stability and good judgment. On board the ship he manufactured out of an old gun barrel and some old lumber, first rate pistols; and from a common cocoa nut, he produced a beautifully carved ornament, for which our captain offered him ten dollars, but he refused. That night a violent storm arose, and dashed into fragments his beautiful workmanship. This clever genius, soon after he landed in San Francisco, found employment as a house and sign painter at eight dollars a day and his board; at night he could earn twice as much in manufacturing rings, breastpins and "specimens." In a short time he had accumulated about $1,500, and concluded he would return home. Intimate as I was with him, knowing thoroughly his circumstances, his prospects and opportunities for accumulating a competency, I entreated, I besought him to remain at least a year longer, but it was of no avail. Off he went, and when, I last heard of him, he was at home sure enough—but was not the possessor of five dollars!

Another passenger, of fine scholastic attainments, was bar-keeper in a gambling saloon. Another was lamp-lighter and watchman in the same house. Another of prepossessing appearance and manners, found employment in a restaurant as a waiter; and another became a prominent actor on the stage.

San Francisco was looming up—elegant stores were established—virtuous women were occasionally met with in the streets, but more frequently women of abandoned principles—good men and bad men were fast coming in—houses were in demand, and the city was rapidly extending. Steamboats plied the placid waters, and no wonder the Indian sighed for the days that were past, for then these "smoke ships" were not there to frighten off the fish.

The Chinese, every man of whom answered to the name of John, began to arrive in considerable numbers. They appeared to be a harmless, inanimate set of beings, and when you saw one of them, you saw the whole race—so remarkably similar are their prominent features.

A large number of French people were flocking in also; and in passing along the Plaza one morning, I observed Monsieur Tonson blacking the boots of some of the sporting fraternity. And I doubt not Mr. Parlezvous Frenchman drove a flourishing business, for he had no rent nor taxes to pay, but with only a stool, his brush and blacking, he would stand on the pavement, and inquire if any " von gentlemen would have ze boots black?"

In truth, representatives of almost every nation, bringing with them all their national prejudices and peculiarities, were fast adding to the population of the state.

Even at this early period of the history of San Francisco, not only the comforts, but many of the luxuries of life could be obtained. The high prices demanded for every description of goods, incited energetic men to push ahead with untiring exertions to produce something likely to be called for. The streets were gradually being planked; some of the houses were quite pretty, and men seemed to feel more cheerful now that the rainy season had passed by, and the prospects for the future were bright.

My friend W—— was taken suddenly ill; his partner had gone to the mines on business, and the whole duty of managing his complicated affairs devolved upon me. My friend was getting worse, and imagined that no one could nurse him as well as I could; and as troubles never come singly, in walked a tenant and peremptorily demanded a reduction of his rent; and then the clerk demanded his pay, as he wished to leave for the mines; and to cap the climax, a note of $800, due in a couple of days, was handed me. I could not annoy the sick man with business matters, so I had to act upon my own judgment, and that promptly. With the tenant I compromised, after considerable wrangling; but had to pay the importunate clerk out of my own funds, and employed another for his board and a percentage on sales; and settled, very much to my surprise satisfactorily with the gentleman who held the note; and then breathed freer myself.

Our steward had been a law student in New York city, and performed his duties satisfactorily; and the cook was decidedly the handsomest man in the house. Our charges were one dollar for a meal, and one dollar for the privilege of sleeping on the "softest plank." By unremitting attention to business, and unwearied watching of my sick friend, he recovered sufficiently, in the course of several weeks, to leave his room—to walk out and enjoy the pure and invigorating air, and the delightful scenery around the city.

On Wednesday, March 27th, 1850, having completed all my arrangements, I bade a farewell to my friends, and stepping aboard the schooner Susan Farnham, was once more on my way to the mines. Not to the southern, but to the northern portion of California, without any business associates, determined to work alone, risk alone, and live alone. The morning was delightful, the air delicious, and everything promised a comfortable voyage. The captain I found an unusually mild and amiable man for his office. The passengers were all gold hunters, and take them all in all, about as kindly disposed a set of fellows as I could have desired. After we passed Benecia, the Sacramento river, on which we were sailing, continued the same width its entire length. It is a beautiful stream, navigable for steamers and large sized vessels; along the shore on either side the banks were covered with innumerable clusters of varied colored flowers—presenting a most charming view; looking as though some gorgeous tapestry was spread over the undulating hills. What a place for the enthusiast in botany!—what brilliant specimens of as yet, undescribed flowers he could secure! Our schooner was not fitted up with berths for passengers, so we had to lie down on the decks; and when a shower came up, we were sadly put to it, as we were unable to escape the rain, or to secure a shelter.

On Monday evening, April 1st, we reached Sacramento city, and our accommodating captain very obligingly held over for a few hours, to allow passengers to go ashore and take a twilight view of the city. Most of us hurried to a large commodious-looking hotel, convenient to the landing, for we had not partaken of a regular meal for nearly a week. After a hearty supper, we strolled around the city, and, so far as we could judge, the ground around was perfectly level.

The wildest excitement was prevailing. An election for municipal officers was about to be held, and processions of the friends of the opposing candidates were parading the streets. I could almost fancy myself in New York. We soon, tired of the excitement, sought the vessel, and were again sailing on our voyage to the gold regions.

On Friday afternoon we anchored awhile at a place called Vernon, where we bought bread for forty cents a loaf. Opposite to this speculating village, on the other shore, was the city of Fremont.

Next morning, about 9 o'clock, Nicholaus hove in sight, at which place a portion of the passengers, including myself, landed, and bade adieu to the friendly captain and crew of the Susan Farnham, who continued on their way, bound far up the Feather river.

I had a letter to a citizen of Nicholaus, and lost no time in conveying my baggage to one of his houses, which at that time was unoccupied, and here we rested several days.

CHAPTER XI.

ON THE MARCH—NEVADA MINES—LIFE IN THE MOUNTAINS—1850.

The town of Nicholaus was pleasantly located on the Feather river, and even at that early period speculators were busy at work buying and selling "town lots." It derived its name from an old man named Nichols, to whom Capt. Sutter presented the ground. Accustomed to living among the Indians, he preferred their free and easy life to a residence within the limits of a town, even though that town bore his name. The old man could neither read nor write, and I subsequently understood that his "friends" were fast disposing of his town lots in a way that he would be compelled to cry out, "Save me from my friends."

On Monday, April 8th, I succeeded in procuring a conveyance to the Nevada Mines for my tent, rocker, mining tools, clothes and bedding, which weighed 111 lbs, and for which I was charged 25 cents per pound—the distance about fifty miles. Being the close of the rainy season, the numerous creeks usually small and shallow, were now deep and rapid rivers, often impeding our progress; and we had not proceeded far out of Nicholaus before we were compelled to unpack our goods, and place them in a boat, and row across one of them. I felt little troubled at these delays, and in truth, began to like this wild, roving and exciting life, especially as I enjoyed excellent health. As I was "all alone" in my business operations, I had none of those unpleasant annoyances to which I was constantly subjected on my trip to the southern mines.— Our party consisted of about a dozen young men, each one of whom hoped that this expedition to the mines would not only be successful, but that the time for returning home would soon arrive.

We came to a small stream called Bear] river, across which a rude bridge had been thrown, and for the privilege of crossing each man was charged 25 cents. We halted for the night a little beyond this, and as the air was fresh and cool, it required considerable management on my part to keep myself comfortable; I slept under the wagon, and used a block of wood for my pillow. Morning ushered in a lovely day—the clouds had disappeared, and we went on our way rejoicing; and why not?—a beautiful day, beautiful scenery and beautiful flowers along our path. About noon we espied a house, and were agreeably surprised to find among its inmates several females, who informed us that their intention was to conduct a "traveler's rest," and cheerfully prepared a substantial dinner for several of our party, each one of whom did full justice to the excellent repast spread before them. We passed on, met several Indians returning from a hunt, all of them in a state of nudity, and their first demand was "bacca, bacca." We gave them as much of the "weed" as we could spare, and away they scampered "over the hills and far away."

About noon on Wednesday 10th, 1850, we reached Rough and Ready—a more appropriately named place could not be found; here we rested awhile and dined — Next day reached Grass Valley, then containing only a couple of log huts and a few tents scattered here and there. [Of this valley I shall speak more particularly in future, for here I enjoyed more real happiness than had ever fallen to my lot in my previous life.] There being nothing particularly interesting to me about here, I leisurely proceeded until I reached the celebrated "Nevada Dry Diggings." Here I pitched my tent and remained a considerable time and lived very pleasantly, although I had many hardships to endure, and was deprived of many of the comforts of life.

An old gentleman, I met here, with whom I had traveled to California, who was anxiously awaiting the arrival of his party, that were to mine and live with him. As he had no tent or mining tools, I invited him to stay with me until his party arrived. I found my friend very useful; I know I could not so easily have erected my tent, or put my mining tools in such complete order, had I not met my obliging acquaintance.

My first purchase was 19 lbs. of salt pork for $7 60, and 5 lbs. flour for $1 75. As wood cost nothing but the trouble of cutting and bringing it to the tent, and as water, pure and wholesome, could be had within a stone's throw of my new home, I soon built a fire, and in a short time my friend and myself were seated on a log, feasting as happily as princes on "salt pork and slap jacks." That night we slept soundly. The next day we "prospected," and entertained an acquaintance at dinner.

On Saturday I devoted most of the day to the arrangement of my tent, and putting my *extensive* establishment in as complete order as possible. I am glad to say that most of the American miners ceased work on the Sabbath. The pine and oak trees in the northern mines grow to a great height, unlike the dwarf oak trees peculiar to the southern mines. The gold about this locality was more generally diffused than in the southern, making the chances for success by individual miners more sure; but perhaps, as I happened to meet with more agreeable acquaintances, and my time passed away more pleasantly, I may be prejudiced in my feelings and opinions as to the relative merits of the northern and southern mines. Mr. C. and I continued working together until April 21st, when his friends arrived, nearly every one of whom I found had been my fellow travelers to California, which was very gratifying to me. Although I missed the old gentleman, particularly at night, I had the whole party with me nearly every evening. My tent appeared to be the attractive spot for very many of the miners, who assembled every evening around the blazing fire I kept up, and I shall ever remember with pleasure the pleasant evenings on that mountain, overlooking the rapidly increasing city of Nevada.

The mines extended over a considerable space of ground. "Gold Run" was the most valuable locality for mining;—immense quantities of the precious metal were taken from it. Other ravines in the neighborhood of Nevada were alive with men digging, washing and panning out the gold.

A company of Frenchmen pitched their tent near mine, and every evening they would make the woods re-echo with their French songs and boisterous merriment. On Sunday evenings they would sing the Marseillaise Hymn, and liquor was the active stimulus to their naturally volatile dispositions.

A little way above me were three Germans. They had no tent, but encamped under a large oak, and these men would call up a melancholy feeling whenever they sang, for their favorite airs were the plaintive, home feeling songs of their Fatherland, after singing which, they would quietly lay down to rest, and silence reigned around.

Nevada was situated in a valley, surrounded by hills

and creeks. Deer Creek was the most important stream, and even this beautiful transparent river was turned from its natural course; in truth the very heart of the city was dug up, and there was no telling where the digging would end.

As usual at every village, the sporting fraternity were on hand, and even in the wilds of California, amid volcanic looking rocks and crevices, where the thunder seemed to roar the loudest, where the lightning flashed most vividly,—there even men who were strangers to the christian religion and its benign influence would congregate, open their games, surrounded by all the paraphernalia of their profession, and entice the unwary, as a " spider does the fly," into their meshes. But there were also men at Nevada who had been accustomed to religious exercises at home—men who had assisted at prayer meetings, who had often prayed, "Lead us not into temptation," and here they conducted themselves so differently that their previous life appeared all a sham.

Very near my tent was located a valued friend from Providence, R. I. This gentleman was a sincere christian and always lived up to his profession. Often when the hard day's work was done, when the night was dark and gloomy, when the only light visible was reflected from a gambling saloon, we would sit down under the umbrageous branches of a tall oak, before a cheerful fire, and sing

the old hymn tunes, so familiar to me from having, when
a boy, joined in singing, in youthful innocence, the same
tunes in the catechetical class. It was not strange that
our ordinary singing would quiet the tumultuous crowd,
for " Old Hundred" would always bring to mind " the
light of other days," and it was not strange, then, that
our locality upon the " hill top" was the " rendezvous' of
a large number of miners.

Another dear friend was Col. C., formerly of Kentucky,
a gentleman of the old school, of fine commanding appearance—his silvery hair only adding dignity to his elegant
contour. He was engaged in merchandizing. When the
days's work over, I always felt tired and jaded. On my
way to my tent, which was near the colonel's store, I
could see the kind and considerate old gentleman watching for my return, always having some refreshment prepared for me. These little acts of kindness endeared
him to me, and it afforded me great pleasure to assist him
at evening in waiting upon his customers.

When we left our tents we always felt sure our valuables would be safe, because the miner's law was *the* law,
and their justice was meted out quick and sure—no quibbling and tedious wrangling. I have seen, at a distance,
men flogged for committing crimes, and then drummed out
of camp. Was a miner robbed, was a miner murdered,
the report flew around the camp with lightning speed.—

The culprit, if caught, was summarily dealth with ; and if persons think this harsh and cruel, they must only place themselves in a country without laws, without proper courts of justice, and then "circumstances alter cases."

Gold hunting is, without doubt, the most exciting life a man can lead. No matter how unsuccessful, no matter if the result of a hard day's labor yielded barely sufficient to pay necessary expenses, the hope, the pleasurable hope of finding the "big lump" next day, fills the miner's breast with joy and delightful anticipation, and keeps up the spirits of men who otherwise would despond. The "pleasures of hope" are more strikingly exemplified in a California miner's life than under any other circumstances.

The whole business is a lottery. Men would sometimes stumble over places, as if by chance, and dig away and secure "a pile." I have been tolerably successful myself, by the merest chance of "prospecting" where others had often and often passed over, without the slightest encouragement to believe that gold could be found there. The success of a miner depends, in a great measure, upon first learning that "a rolling stone gathers no moss." Too often men would leave good locations, actuated by an uncontrollable restlessness, and such would rarely succeed. But those that were content to work steadily, "mind their own business," and resist temptation, generally reaped the greatest reward in gold digging.

Physical strength was all-important. Men with stout arms, who could handle the pick and shovel all day, and retain their health, were most successful. I know that if my physical strength had equaled my disposition and will to work, I should soon have secured a competency.

CHAPTER XII.
A PEDESTRIAN EXCURSION TO WASHINGTON CITY—INCIDENTS AT THE MINES, &c., &c.—1850.

The rain had ceased—the dark and threatening clouds had disappeared—the small streams were fast drying up—the dews no longer moistened the parched earth, and hillside and valley looked as dry as though the rain had never descended. The almost, if not entirely, perpetual snow that capped the towering mountains of the Sierra Nevada, yielded slightly to the noon-day heat, and thus the various streams contiguous, were sustained.

Men who had journeys to perform of any distance, always carried a supply of water with them; and yet one of the peculiarities of the climate was, that no matter how hot and oppressive the sun's rays, the moment you could find shelter under a tree, the air was cool and delicious, owing to the constant breeze from the surrounding mountains.

My friend from Rhode Island was anxious to visit "Washington city," situated on the Yuba river, distant about twenty-five miles; and, as he knew I was always ready for a tramp, and desirous of seeing as much of the country as possible, proposed that I should accompany him. So, on Thursday, May 30th, we commenced our march in fine humor and excellent condition—like most travelers afoot, we were talking and laughing as merrily as school boys, until we began to ascend the first mountain on our way, and then didn't we toil and pant? Not a word was now spoken; slowly we pressed on, and when we reached the summit of the rugged mountain we were bathed in perspiration. We had our bedding strapped to our backs, the rays of the sun were beating down upon us, and I began to think, that I at least was paying "dear for the whistle." When about midway to our journey's end, my friend fainted, and fell by the roadside. I was in a pretty predicament, not a drop of water by me, and none in sight; so I sat by him till he revived. He determined to continue on; I insisted upon carrying his pack, and we traveled along pretty well for a mile or more, when over he tumbled again; this time I sought around in various directions for water, but none could I perceive, and when I returned to him he was sitting up, ready to proceed—so on we marched.

At length I espied a path diverging from the main road,

and following it we found a cool spring, where we quenched our thirst, washed our faces, and felt much refreshed. Again we started forward, and soon came to the wildest, and most romantic natural scenery I had ever beheld. Imagine two mountains cleft asunder, a rugged wall of rocks and rubbish rising in the middle of the gap to the top, forming a natural causeway from one mountain to the other. On either side a valley so deep that it pained the eye to gaze down so far. There were evidences of some violent concussion of nature—some terrible volcanic eruption, which had torn the rocks asunder—piled them in pyramidal form, while here and there huge boulders stood out alone, and the very earth we passed over seemed to be ground pumice stone. Pausing awhile to gaze in silent awe upon this grand spectacle, we passed on, still seeming to ascend higher and higher the long range of mountains, and occasionally we obtained an uninterrupted view of the magnificent and diversified scenery around us.

Here we could perceive the North Yuba river rushing madly down the precipitous rocks. Again, further on, some vast plain where the foot of white man had never yet trod; and yonder to the right of us were the Sierra Nevada mountains, their lofty summits almost lost to view amid the clouds.

We began to think if Washington was only twenty-five miles from Nevada, it was time we were within sight of it.

On ascending another rock we perceived something like a village before us; we pressed forward, but we thought our progress must be either very slow, or else the path we were pursuing only wound round and round the gigantic mountain. We were exceedingly thirsty, continually crying out for water! water! and what annoyed us the more was, the sight of a clear stream of mountain water coursing rapidly down the rugged rocks and cliffs, but inaccessible to us.

So steep was this mountain that wagons, loaded with provisions for the miners about Washington, had large trees fastened to their wheels, and with a push they were started forward and allowed to bring up wherever they could. Oftentimes they upset, scattering flour, bacon and rum in beautiful confusion over the ground. We finally reached the foot of the mountain, and gladly sat down beneath a tall oak to rest. My friend's acquaintances were located upon the opposite side of the river, upon whose banks we were resting. Towards dusk we started forward, crossed over the river on a log, and after considerable difficulty in following the tortuous path, found the friends we were in search of. We were too weary even for conversation, and reserved our observations on claims and mining until morning, and found comfort in a good night's rest on the moss-covered rocks, peeping out here and there like cannon on some ancient fort.

The next morning I enjoyed a refreshing bath in the river, and after locating claims, recrossed the Yuba, and partook of a capital breakfast at the "Washington House." We took a view of the mining operations, but I was so dissatisfied with the locality that I cordially seconded my friend's proposal to proceed homeward the following morning. The result of my trip amounted to nothing, for I never thought of my claims one day afterwards, although I was importuned to "come up and assist in getting out the ore."

On Saturday, June 1st, we slowly reascended the rough and precipitous mountain, and when we sat down to rest, found we had consumed a great part of the morning in the ascent. The scenery appeared even more picturesque than on our first day's tramp, but as we were returning home and knew the route better, we may have felt more inclined to observe and enjoy the varied beauties of the country. Sometimes our road was perfectly level; then ascended a steep mountain, overlooking an almost interminable space of ground, and again it seemed lost in a woods, thickly studded with lofty trees of gigantic dimensions, where the almost oppressive silence was disturbed only by the sweet carols of the numerous beautiful birds, that were flying above and around us.

The extreme heat of the sun, our blistered feet, and wearied limbs, caused us very frequently to halt and rest.

Occasionally, other parties overtook us, and the grotesque appearance we mutually presented, afforded merriment to all. Twilight was setting in, and our march was enlivened by the music of the myriads of insects that keep quiet during the light of day, but swarm around at night. We were nearly overcome with fatigue, and proposed resting for the night on the road, when some one espied the lights reflected from the city, and we pushed forward and soon arrived safely at our tents, where we met with a cordial reception from our friends.

That night I slept so soundly that a volley from a regiment of soldiers only could have awakened me, nor did I awake from my slumbers until the sun introduced another day, and the many birds that always perched on the branches of trees near me, were singing their morning songs.

I rested for several days with all the "*otium cum dignitate*" of a prince, under the beautiful trees that sheltered my mountain home; and not until I fully recovered my usual strength did I venture to resume gold hunting.

I was engaged at the "intellectual" occupation of *frying sweet cakes*, when I happened to look up, and perceived a woman, fatigued and care-worn, propounding questions to me about Nevada and the best place to pitch her tent; she told me her husband, driving a "wagon and two," was on his way, and she desired to select a location prior to his arrival. I had been listening so attentively to the lady that, upon looking at my cakes, I found not only them, but the leaves around, were burning up, and thus my " extra dish" was lost! However, I selected a delightfully shaded spot for the stranger to locate, and in a short time the husband drove along, and thus another tent was added to the hill. We had lived so many months without the refining influence of respectable women, that each of us felt glad to see our town improving, and women being added to the large crowd of men who needed something to restrain them in their frolics and boisterous conduct. And yet I had become so accustomed to the wild, free and unrestrained life of a California miner, that I must confess I felt uncomfortable to find my heretofore quiet retreat upon the " hill top," invaded by strangers, thus destroying, as it were, my privacy and solitude.

One great disadvantage we labored under was the difficulty of procuring our letters from San Francisco; until, finally, two men started an express, and for two dollars they would bring a letter, provided, of course, there were any there for us. I know I did not add to their treasury, for either my friends did not trouble themselves to write to me, or else the void my absence created was soon filled; at all events, the express men invariably informed me—" nothing for you, sir." The only satisfaction

I had was in finding fault with "Uncle Sam" and his whole batch of clerks.

Among my evening visitors were several young men, whose tent was nearly a mile from mine, and they reported one evening that "something was going on" about their locality;—that "men who had valuable claims were packing up their mining tools," and if they had not some better claims in view, they certainly would not forsake those they were working.

I hardly knew how to account for this, but we separated with the understanding that each man would seek all the information he could, and report next evening. For myself, I only casually heard of "rich mining districts," located far up the mountains, but could obtain no positive information. The next evening I had a blazing fire burning, and my Rhode Island friend and myself were seated on the old log, in front of my tent, awaiting our "up river friends." At length, all were assembled together, and now for the news. " Well," began the most enthusiastic miner, " I have the whole secret; a man has returned from a distant place exhibiting considerable gold dust, and he wants fifty reliable men, each to be supplied with three month's provisions, to purchase two mules to carry mining utensils and supplies, and he will take them to the Gold Lake, where the richest deposits of gold can be found; and if his declarations should not hold good, his life to pay the forfeit. '

This was exciting intelligence to us, and as the "mule party," as we termed them, kept their plans secret, and intended to go off at night, we agreed to follow after them "on foot," and determined to come in for a share. The excitement, I found, was extending. Our party of *bold and determined men* fixed the time for starting, and in the next chapter I will give a report of our journey in search of "Gold Lake."

CHAPTER XIII.
THE GOLD LAKE EXPEDITION.

On Friday, June 7th, 1850, there might have been observed, here and there, a number of men with large packs on their backs, slowly wending their way over the precipitous hills surrounding Nevada, and not until they entered upon the lovely valley about three miles distant, did they halt and make their final arrangements for the arduous expedition they were about to undertake. The advance party was provided with mules, and their movements were kept secret; and although we were traveling on foot, we always managed to hold our own with them. The first day's tramp brought us to "Washington"— described in a former chapter. We encamped under the sheltering branches of a venerable oak, but we rested badly;—our limbs were so sore and bruised, that when we arose in the morning, we were more fit for a bed than for travel over the worst roads that can be imagined.

Saturday, June 8th, we crossed the Yuba river on a log which the miners had thrown across for their convenience; and as the river was wide, and the waters rolling rapidly, the greatest caution was necessary to save us from a tumble into the stream. Our packs were becoming too burdensome, and I gave away, as did others, such articles as I did not absolutely require. We came to "Poor Man's Creek," so called, in consequence of some miners who had been unsuccessful in other localities taking up claims here.— This stream coursed along the gap of the rugged mountain that seemed to hide it from view; and the climbing of the steep and rough hill on the other side of it almost exhausted the party who where bound for Gold Lake.

On we pressed; sometimes we had to force our way through low chaparral, whose thorny stems interlaced each other, tearing our clothes and persons, and then, again, wading through rapid streams as straight in their course as the twists of the numerous serpents we passed. Towards night we ascended another steep and rugged mountain, from whose summit we saw the Middle Yuba; and when we succeeded in crossing this narrow but angry stream, we found a valley of limited size, where we encamped for the night.

The mountains over which we had traveled were heavily

timbered with oak, pine and cedar trees. Although the days were uncomfortably warm, the nights were very cool. I was much refreshed by a cold bath in the river. Here I found an old man selling flour. I purchased 12½ pounds of flour, for which the old settler charged *only* $5 75.— His account of the road before us was any thing but encouraging. After cooking and eating a very meagre supper, I sought my blankets, and slept as soundly as the rock-bound hills.

Sunday, June 9th. We started on our "Goose lake expedition," as we now began to term it, long before the sun had appeared above the lofty hills, and such a road for a man to travel, to say nothing of the great weight each one carried on his back! We now began to lose sight of rivers, creeks and rivulets, and suffered much for the want of water. My experience has taught me that the absence of food is not near so distressing as the deprivation of water.

We scarcely uttered a word, and our tongues protruded, and often I would hear some one cry out, "is there no water near!" This day's tramp exceeded all the hardships I had yet undergone, but we were agreeably surprised to find at its terminus quite a village. We had reached the north fork of Yuba river, near which was located the city of Downieville, which has since become an important place. Here we had a capital supper, charge $2, after which we sought our comfortable blankets, and slept as usual under the friendly branches of one of the numerous trees abounding here.

Monday, June 10th. After breakfast at the "French Restaurant," I purchased two pounds of ham for $2 25.— This, with my flour, cooking utensils, mining implements, clothing and bedding, were strapped to my back—a load more fit for a mule than a human being to carry.

As usual, we were early on the start, and I did not wonder at the miners around here, regarding with wonder and surprise, the almost fagged out, but determined party. Passing them by, on we went, and soon found another stupendous mountain in our road, and I began to think if we ascended many more such mountains we would reach the clouds. The change in the temperature was very perceptible; when we arrived at the summit snow was seen ahead of us. Our feelings were not so gay as when we started, but still we endeavored to cheer each other, hoping that "Gold Lake" would be reached before long. Other parties, we understood, were following us, and the excitement throughout the State was increasing. On we plodded until we came to hills covered with snow, which led us to suppose we were getting into a region of perpetual snow. Finding a clear, dry spot of ground, we encamped. As we had been unable to carry an abundant supply of provisions, each man ate sparingly. After putting on the fire all the old stumps and logs we could find, we stretched our blankets on the ground, and, as usual, slept comfortably.

Tuesday, June 11th. The air was chilly, and the appearance of the road ahead by no means cheering; the snow had nearly filled up the valleys, and as far as the eye could reach, the earth seemed clothed in the same wintery garb, and for the first time in our pilgrimage, we began to fear that we had lost our reckoning of the probable latitude of Gold Lake.

We sat down upon the hard frozen snow, and endeavored to study out whether we were going to, or from the coveted lake. Far away over the mountains we could see the lurid smoke arising from the wigwam of the hostile Indian. The only tracks we could perceive were the footprints of deer and bears; and each man, but myself, (as I carried no weapon) examined his gun and prepared for the worst.

At length we decided to proceed in a northerly direction, and began the ascent of another mountain; after awhile, on looking up, we thought we saw on the summit the ruins of some old castle or monastery, but when we reached the top of the mountain, we found that what we supposed to be some ancient ruin, was nothing but huge boulders projecting from the highest point of the mountain. We found the valley on the other side, filled to the tops of tall pine trees with snow, and we were puzzled how to proceed, until we finally hit upon the laughable expedient of each man placing his wash pan on the snow, then getting into it, and with a gentle shove, down we went pell mell, over and over, rolling and tumbling, until we reached the base. Here we had unmistakable evidence that we were in the track of the party in advance; so on we traveled. We came to a wild looking place, interspersed with ravines and valleys, stretched along the base of the high mountains, which we afterwards learned constituted "Canon creek and valley."

We rested in the valley which was free from snow, and partook of a *very cold* collation. My feet were wet, my shoulders sore, I felt in no very agreeable mood, although I was assured by my companions that my cheerful conversation kept them in excellent spirits. There was an elderly man with us, and I feared he could not endure the deprivations and exposures he was necessarily forced to undergo, and for his sake, I exerted myself to appear gay and lively. On we tramped, crossing snow banks, then getting almost bewildered in a dense forest, and again emerging on a plain of dreary, cheerless snow. Still on, on we pressed, until the straps of my bundle gave way, and I determined to halt until I could repair them. They had lacerated my shoulders, and produced intense pain. Well for the jaded and unhappy men that I was compelled to halt, for we had not been long seated ere we heard the tinkling of a bell. "What is that?" "Can it be the approach of hostile Indians?" "Come, men, shoulder arms! let us prepare to act on the defensive." Just then, from around a hill of snow, was observed, slowly approaching, a man leading a mule, to which was attached a bell! then another, and another, and we discovered that, instead of hostile Indians, they were the advance party returning from their " Goose lake hunt!" They reported the utter impossibility of proceeding farther, in consequence of the interminable mountains of snow; that they believed the snow about here was perpetual.

They were accompanied by the man who betrayed and disappointed them; and while some of the party clamored for his death, the rest, more kindly and charitably disposed, begged for his life, believing that his reason was dethroned! The party passed on, and as they carried their mining implements with them, we believed their story.

When they were out of sight, all around us was still and quiet, save the chilling winds, howling through the almost impenetrable forests. We, seven men, feeling the importance of our lonely and isolated situation, held counsel together, and agreed to retrace our steps after breakfast next morning. Every one of us felt serious and solemn; our consultation was conducted with more solemnity than any meeting I had ever attended before.

Wednesday, June 12th. Although a blazing fire was kept up, the air was so keen that we could not keep comfortable with our scanty bedding. We breakfasted on bread baked in the ashes, without salt or saleratus; we gnawed at a bone, from which the meat had disappeared a day or two previously; and drank tea made of spruce twigs. Although disappointed in our anticipations, although we endured almost incredible hardships, still we were content; we risked our lives and comfort to be sure, but we started to California to better our fortunes, and in pursuit of the same object, we started on this expedition with the hope of accumulating "our pile" in little "less than no time." After our meagre breakfast we started on our return to Nevada. We met other parties bound for Gold Lake, and all our representations and persuasions could not influence them. On they went, only to certain disappointment.

Night came on—dark dreary night, among the snow clad hills, and again we halted, constructed a bush arbor, threw our aching limbs upon the ground, and slept "until daylight did appear."

Thursday, June 13th. Cloudy when we started; after awhile a cold chilly rain set in, and we were all completely saturated. Some were suffering greatly from the effects of the cold and damp atmosphere. Towards noon we concluded to halt, and wait for the storm to cease.

Friday, June 14th. Rested badly last night, and as the storm of rain and sleet continued, and further travel would be impossible, we concluded to remain here, and at once commenced the erection of a temporary shelter by cutting down saplings and gathering brush, and when our *magnificent* structure was completed, we hoped we had secured for that night a comfortable rest. We started a fire—piled on old logs and stumps, and if the snow had not served as a barrier, we might have fired the woods.— After *supper* we laid down to court the sleep we so much needed.

Saturday, June 15th. While the storm was at its highest, when the snow, rain, hail and wind appeared to be violently contending for the mastery, the night as dark as Erebus, down tumbled our "splendid bush arbor!"— Drenched to the skin and half frozen, we scrambled from under the cold, wet bushes, stirred up the almost dying embers, and with the patience of Job, stood around a blazing fire, endeavoring to dry our bed and baggage.— We hugged around the fire like half frozen Indians, until daylight appeared. And as the storm continued, we began to think we were in a latitude that knew no fair weather, so we bundled up our partially dried clothes, and determined to proceed onward, for surely, we could hardly fare worse. We traveled Indian fashion—one behind the other, and when we had proceeded about four or five miles, we were agreeably surprised to find the sun shining and not a particle of snow visible. We now felt more comfortable, and towards night came in sight of Downieville. At last we reached the settlement, and after partaking of a refreshing meal at the "French Hotel," we sought our blankets and enjoyed a good night's rest.

CHAPTER XIV.
CONCLUSION OF THE GOLD LAKE EXPEDITION—MINES AND MINING ABOUT NEVADA.—1850.

The next day feeling somewhat rested, we took a stroll through the village of Downieville. Here, far away from any other settlement—high up in the mountains—where a few months previous, white man had never trod; where the untutored Indian hunted the numerous wild animals prowling around; where the clear, almost transparent river had followed its meandering course for ages undisturbed, the country now teemed with brave, energetic and persevering Americans, who had driven back the hostile and trifling Indian, turned the river from its natural channel, and were building up a town, which promised to become of considerable importance. When this country belonged to the thriftless and indifferent Mexican, these hills and valleys lavished upon the desert air their wealth and beauty. It remained for the indomitable and thorough-going Anglo-Saxon race, to bring forth the mineral and agricultural wealth of this beautiful and valuable country.

About the time I am writing, Downieville numbered some five hundred inhabitants, but there were many miners who lived in their own tents outside the village.

The steep and lofty mountain directly fronting the little village of tents, was so rugged and sudden in its declivity, that wagons could not descend; hence, mules packed with about 200 lbs. of provisions were started ahead, and sometimes, cautious in his step as this animal is known to be, he would miss his foothold, tumble over and over, until he reached the base, and not unfrequently plunge into the river, where the poor beast found rest in death. I had a sufficient supply of flour to last me for two or three days, but tired of my meagre fare, I purchased $1\frac{1}{2}$ lbs. of salt pork for $1 13; fried out the fat, and made bread " so rich," that hungry as I was, I could scarcely swallow it.

Monday, June 17th. Early in the morning we "hitched up" our packs, bade farewell to Downieville, and resumed our home-bound tramp. After suffering great fatigue, and almost incredible hardships, we reached the "middle Yuba station" about dusk. I enjoyed a capital bath in the river, and having partaken of a *very light supper*, I " turned in" my blankets, and regardless of the many wild animals that were prowling around and had never " smelt gun-powder," I soon forgot my weariness in refreshing sleep.

Tuesday, June 18th. Slept comfortably last night, and after breakfast—and such a breakfast! we shouldered our packs, crossed the river, and pursued a different route from the one we traveled on our upward trip. We ascended a hill beautifully shaded by oak, cedar and pine trees, and the view, as far around as the eye could reach, was charming. About noon we reached Poor Man's Creek; here we found a man selling refreshments under a bush arbor, and after encouraging the newly established caterer, for the inner man, we shouldered arms, (I was going to say,) but packs, I mean, and commenced the ascent of a mountain so steep, that we were often compelled to seize hold of the low bushes growing here and there, to prevent our falling backward. This was an exceedingly tedious and wearisome exercise, as most of it was performed on all fours; but a rest on the brow of the mountain, shaded by lofty oaks, and a delightful breeze prevailing, refreshed us very much. We were soon again on the march, and "trotted down the hill" much faster than we had climbed up on the other side.

Late in the day, we espied the "great mountain city of Washington," and although we had no acquaintances there to welcome our arrival, still the fact that we were approaching a familiar spot, made us feel much more agreeable than when we halted at other places further up the mountains.

We refreshed ourselves by a capital supper, and an invigorating bath in the Yuba river, which coursed along, not only the villages, but rushed rapidly down the gaps of the steep, rugged and high mountains, so peculiar to the extreme northern portion of California.

Wednesday, June 19th. At early dawn, when the sun was just peeping above the lofty hills surrounding Washington, our bodies strengthened and spirits enlivened by the pure and invigorating mountain air, we commenced another day's tramp. We avoided climbing the stupendous mountain crossed on our first day's march, by following a zig-zag path, which ran along the river, until it reached the village of Jefferson, and was there lost in a labyrinth of rocks, bushes and briers, which defied the efforts of man to disentangle. "Jefferson city," boasting of only a tent or two, and holding out no inducements for jaded passengers to stop and contemplate, we pushed ahead, hoping to reach Nevada by night. To our delight, we found a mountain cottage in our path, a comfortable tenement erected since we had passed along a few days previous. Here we appeased our hunger and quenched our thirst with the cool, sparkling water, gushing up from beneath a tall, straight oak, and again pushed ahead, feeling very comfortable and in good humor with ourselves and all around us.

The roads were now more level, the temperature delightful. Difficult, arduous, and pecuniarily unprofitable as our expedition had proved, nevertheless, the prospect of soon reaching our tents and enjoying a rest, and of once more meeting our Nevada friends, filled our hearts with unalloyed pleasure. On we plodded, and it was not strange that we fancied the very trees we passed, the very grass we trod down, appeared more pleasing to the eye than when we traveled over the same road a few days previously. The next stopping place was the " Franklin House ;" here we likewise partook of refreshments. The Franklin was only a blue tent, but it afforded a very acceptable shelter from the rays of the sun. The scenery around was beautiful, not such stupendous mountains, not such rugged paths as we had recently passed over, but presenting in admirable contrast, a lovely open country. We " up packs" and leisurely proceeded until we reached the *formidable* Rock Creek, a stream about six inches deep, and about forty inches wide; and after a cooling draught and a comfortable rest on the green sward, we resumed our march, and before dark espied our tents standing out like sentinels on the hill top, seeming to invite us to come and take possession ; of course, our acquaintances congregated around us that night, and the shouts of laughter that our description of Gold Lake hunting called forth, were loud enough to awaken the numerous birds that found shelter in the trees above us.

Thursday, June 20th. As an evidence of the continued high prices of the necessaries of life, I will enumerate what I purchased this day—35 cts. for ¼ lb. saleratus; 25 cts. for ½ lb. salt; $2 for 20 lbs. of flour; $1 60 for 4 lbs. salt pork; and 50 cts for one pint of molasses.

The journey from which I had just returned, although yielding no pecuniary advantage, still afforded me the best opportunity of observing the upper country of California, which very few at that time had ventured to explore.

The scenery along the route was most grand, oftentimes sublime; the trees which predominated were the cedar, spruce, pine and oak, generally of immense size and height. The flowers were chiefly wild roses, jessamine, and the humble, but sweet scented violet. Very frequently we made tea out of spruce twigs, which, if not possessing any stimulating properties, at least had a pleasant taste, not unlike lemonade. Our meat, so long as we had any, was roasted on a stick, and our bread baked in the ashes. Squirrels and small birds were numerous; grizzly bear tracks were often seen, and as for snakes, we met them far more frequently than we desired.

On Thursday, June 28th, I commenced work in earnest, and so long as my physical strength held out, I continued remarkably successful, and what was equally remarkable, every member of our party on the Gold Lake expedition succeeded in procuring profitable claims. In a previous chapter I ventured the opinion that in most cases success in gold hunting was a mere lottery, and as an exemplification of that assertion, I will cite my claim on Gold run. I had rested several days after my return from my arduous journey, and began to feel a disposition to resume work, so I threw my shovel and wash-pan over my shoulder, and started out on a prospecting tour. I followed along Gold run for a mile or more, and although there were no evidences of valuable "dirt" to wash, I concluded I would make an attempt here, where the lofty pines afforded a delightful shade, and a short distance below a beautiful running spring, which seemed to say, "come and try me." I washed out a couple of pans of dirt, and I felt satisfied I had found my fortune at last. Off I scampered to my tent, offered a man who was complaining of "nothing to do," half of the day's proceeds; and we hurried over to Gold run with my rocker and mining tools. It was not long before we were digging, rattling, and splashing away at a brisk rate. The weather was extremely warm, but the shade from the lofty pines sheltered us, and the little spring was a treasure. That night we divided twenty-four dollars, and had not yet reached the richest deposits.— Next day, before the stars had passed out of sight, we were cooking our breakfast, and before the sun had come forth, we were hard at work.

My claim continued to "pay well" and increase in

value, and this hitherto deserted spot was becoming crowded with gold hunters, digging all around me, but without success; and I continued prospering and "coining money," until the hard labor, too severe for my constitution, enfeebled by my late journey, completely prostrated me, and I was compelled to give up mining. In the meanwhile my claim was "jumped," and in less than a month other parties succeeded in extracting $8,000.

CHAPTER XV.

LEAVING THE MINES—OFF ON A VOYAGE TO THE TROPICS.

Tuesday, July 23d, 1850. Bidding adieu to all my friends about Nevada, I jumped into a covered wagon, and with five other passengers, started for Sacramento. The frequent exposures and hardships to which I had been subjected, told seriously upon my health, and I conceived the idea that a voyage on the "deep blue sea" would restore me to full strength and vigor. On Wednesday, July 24th, we reached a tent, whose proprietor was so genial and accommodating, that we held over until the next day.

Thursday, July 25th. Reached Sacramento about noon. The improvements that had been made since my first visit, about three months previously, attested the assertion I then advanced about the indomitable energy and enterprise of the American settlers. Elegant and commodious houses had been erected, and there were indubitable manifestations that Sacramento would assume a high rank among the cities of California. The city was built upon level ground—in fact, for miles north of it, there was scarcely a hill to be seen, and the admirable water front served as an anchorage for vessels of the largest capacity.

During the afternoon, I stepped aboard a small steamer bound for San Francisco; and after a tedious and rough passage, reached the metropolis of California on Saturday morning, July 27th. Soon after I landed, I received the unpleasant intelligence that my trunk, containing my best clothing, and all my little valuables, had been destroyed by fire during my absence from the city; and the hotel, in which I had enjoyed so many pleasant evenings, was also consumed, together with a vast amount of property adjoining; all of which was the fiendish work of some vile incendiary. I was grieved to learn that nearly every one of my intimate acquaintances had left the city, some for home, and others for different sections of the State.

On Saturday, August 3d, I numbered one among a hundred or more men, treading the decks of the brig Ann and Julia, bound for Panama. A breeze springing up during the afternoon, the anchor was hoisted, and with three cheers from ship and shore, we headed for the tropics. If the Pacific ocean, was named under the impression that it was more mild and less tempestuous than the Atlantic ocean, my experience does not accord with that of Magellan's; for we had an almost continuous succession of storms and rough seas, that tried hard our "A No. 1 coppered and copper fastened brig."

Some of the passengers, tired of a life on the ocean, after a couple of week's experience on board the staunch old brig, prevailed upon the captain to steer for Acapulco, Mexico. I was delighted at this change, for although I had no intention of leaving the vessel, it would give me an opportunity of seeing more places than were put down in the programme. We frequently saw whales, porpoises, and flying fish; and a passenger harpooned a dolphin, a most beautiful fish, weighing at least sixty pounds. When placed upon deck, I watched its expiring death-throes.— It seemed to emulate all the colors of the rainbow, and with its last struggle, it gave a terrible lashing of the deck with its fan-shaped tail.

On the evening of August 13th, we were visited by a terrible gale, which tossed our vessel up and down, as though it had been a chip. The orders of the captain, answered by the crew, only added to the deafening roar of the angry waters; and in the height of the storm, some one cried out, "Man overboard." His awful cry for "help, help, help," was heard above the roar of wind and waves. The ship was almost beyond control; and even if a boat could have been thrown over, it could not have lived two minutes in that dreadful hurricane. And ere we had time to comprehend his hopeless situation, the maddened, upheaving waves had carried the poor fellow beyond reach. I had been conversing with him but a few moments prior to his being knocked overboard, and I regretted exceedingly the loss of one who had braved the hardships and exposures of a miner's life;—one about to return to those who knew and loved him; his heart exulting in the happy anticipation of a speedy union with his betrothed, and for whom, life presented a bright prospect of future happiness and usefulness.

Some days subsequent to this melancholy incident, another passenger was knocked overboard by the "jib boom;" but as the sea was comparatively smooth, and the luckless passenger a good swimmer, he was rescued. I felt painfully excited to see a human being struggling in the ocean, his form receding from the vessel. We feared our long boat could not reach him in time; we all sang out to him, "keep up, keep up." He divested himself of his pantaloons and boots, and struggled manfully against the current, which was carrying him almost out of sight. Sections of masts were thrown overboard, which fortunately reached him. He seized hold of one, and buoyed himself up until the long boat reached him, and he was soon once more on deck.

On Tuesday, August 27th, we neared Acapulco, Mexico; but it always seemed as though, when we were heading for a port, the wind died away. At length, after a slow sail, we espied the Mexican territory; but as Acapulco is hemmed in by high hills, the town was invisible until we rounded a range of rocks, and then it suddenly burst upon our view. The anchor was let go, and such a bustle and confusion as was on board that vessel then, was enough to frighten the lazy, thriftless natives. Row boats, dugouts, and boats of various shapes and sizes, surrounded our vessel, each ladened with tropical fruits, eggs, sweet bread, and milk, and a brisk trade was at once commenced. I did not go ashore until next day, when, accompanied by several friends, we chartered a row boat, and as the distance from the anchorage was short, we were soon landed on Mexican soil. Immediately in front of the principal landing, (there were no wharves,) was a long, one storied stone building, known as the United States Hotel, with the most miserable fare and accommodations. To the right of this building was another tavern, having a drug store in one room—and such a drug store! The street leading from the hotel is wide, well paved, (and the only paved street,) and at its terminus is an old fort, commanding a fine sweep of the bay, but chiefly used as a "calaboose." The houses are principally constructed of reeds and mud, no sash or glass, the roofs of straw. Of course, in these tropical towns, there is no need of chimneys. Crosses are plastered all around the houses, on the doors and gates, and on all the public buildings. No order or regularity is observed in laying out the streets, which, however, are very cleanly; not owing to the energy of the inhabitants, but to natural causes; for through many of the streets flows clear spring water. I noticed a large number of buzzards walking and flying about the town, and I supposed they were the public scavengers.

Some fine cocoanut trees were standing about the place, and I noticed, what appeared remarkable to me, cocoanuts fully ripe, some just budding, and others nearly matured, all on the same tree, which grew to about forty feet in height, with no branches, except at the extreme top, where the fruit clusters. The natives are of a dark complexion, resembling our mulattoes. They appeared civil, social, and fond of strangers. The majority of them were sadly deficient in intellectual acquirements. The soldiers parading about the streets, some of them without boots or shoes, looked not unlike Falstaff's guard. Just in front of the fort I enjoyed a fine bath in the ocean every day that I remained here. The rocks were so worn by the repeated washings of the tide, that in some places they formed excellent substitutes for bathing tubs; and I had capital sport in watching the tide coming in and dashing its briny spray over me. These repeated salt water baths invigorated me, and exercised a sanative influence upon my system, so that I felt inclined for another venture in the wilds of California.

As I remarked, the hotels were miserably conducted; so several of us agreed to enter the best looking house we came across, and ask for accommodations until our ship was ready to set sail. Unfortunately, I was chosen spokesman. Scarce a word of Spanish could any of our party speak or understand. In we went, bowing and scraping— so did the pretty signoritas. I talked Indian, Greek and Chinese, I thought, but not a word that I uttered could the ladies understand. Then the rest made an unsuccessful attempt, until finally the whole party burst out laughing, and I really believe this was the best thing for us; for we soon felt convinced our Mexican friends were willing to accommodate us, when assured we were respectable Americans. I succeeded in telling our hostess that we wanted supper, for which we would willingly pay a liberal price; our object being to escape the crowd of travelers daily arriving—as Acapulco was the most convenient landing place for all steamers and sailing vessels bound to or from California via Panama.

We always slept aboard the ship, and next morning I invited a particular friend, who could speak the Spanish language fluently, to accompany our party to breakfast, at our private hotel. He did so, and told us that the family "had never entertained strangers, but as they supposed the hotels were crowded, and we appeared to be gentlemen, and rather liked our manners, they were glad to entertain us." Obliging as we found our Mexican friends, they were nevertheless exorbitant in their charges. We were satisfied, however, and, I doubt not, had the best fare the place could afford. Our meals consisted of sweetened bread, (no butter,) onions, tomatoes, eggs and coffee; a strange medley, but we relished it. Our captain having completed his arrangements—those of our passengers who had desired to be landed here having started for Vera Cruz— notice was given the remaining passengers "to come aboard," and on Friday, August 30th, we hoisted anchor, spread the sails to the breeze, and headed for Panama; but we had scarcely lost sight of land, before some of the passengers entreated the captain to steer for Realajo, Central America.

As the port charges always amount to considerable, those passengers who preferred stopping at Acapulco and Realajo agreed to pay the expenses;—hence, the captain acquiesced. It was of little consequence to me where we stopped, for I was only journeying for the benefit of my health.

Of all the terrific squalls and storms that I had ever experienced, this sail from Acapulco to Realajo surpassed them all; but a kind Providence protected us, and we safely anchored about six miles from Realajo, (which is as near as vessels can approach,) on Tuesday, Sept. 17th. I noticed a few miles from our anchorage, a burning volcano. On Wednesday I jumped into a dug-out, the halfclad oarsmen gave the signal, lazily bent to their oars, and we slowly rounded towards the village. This was the rainy season, and every now and then we received a "fine ducking," which seemed to delight the natives, but was not so agreeable to their passengers. On our way I observed, standing on the shore, unconcerned and heedless of shouts, a fine specimen of the Iguana, of a light green color and about a yard long, being nothing more than a gigantic lizard. At length we reached the landing, in front of which was a row of one storied, dilapidated buildings in which were the quarters of the soldiers, and also the custom house. The streets were very muddy, and the little children, who were playing in them, enjoying the frequent showers, (and I may say, the plentiful supply of mud,) were naked; and I was told children are allowed to run about until their sixth year without a particle of clothing upon them. As I walked along I thought I perceived a fine apple orchard, but when I approached it, I found it was an orange grove. The houses are built of reeds and mud, with the exception of a few stone edifices, which have the appearance of having stood for centuries. The religion is Roman Catholic. Fruits were cheap and abundant, and board and lodging quite reasonable.

Most of the fencing about this place was formed of the Cactus plant, some of which were twenty feet in height. I remained ashore that night, and must give the numerous gnats, musquitoes, lizards and roaches the credit of being the only industrious inhabitants in the country. The captain left for the city of Leon, the capital of the State, in search of canvas, as we lost our "main sail" in one of the severe gales which we encountered on our voyage here. Every passenger but myself deserted our vessel and crossed the country, bound for the United States.

CHAPTER XVI.

OFF AGAIN—BOUND FOR CALIFORNIA—A GUNNING EXPEDITION.

On Friday, November 8th, 1850, the captain of the staunch old brig, Ann and Julia, came aboard, and declared his determination to set sail for San Francisco, as the intelligence he received from Panama would not warrant his going there, particularly as all the passengers but myself had left the vessel, and I was by no means anxious to sail for Panama, although I had paid my passage thither. So "man the windlass" was ordered, and up came the anchor accompanied by the peculiar singing of the crew.

A fine breeze prevailing, the sails which had lain idle for several weeks were unfurled to the winds, and we headed for the land of gold. Being the only cabin passenger, I enjoyed plenty of state-room accommodations, of which I was debarred on my downward voyage.

The people of Guatemala are, like all other persons living in the tropical climes, wanting in energy, enterprise and "goaheadativeness." I sometimes wondered how the numerous monkeys could be so nimble and active, for in all my travels, I have rarely met with a more indolent set of beings than the natives of Central America. Although their land is of the richest quality, admirably adapted for agricultural purposes, they are too lazy to till the soil, allowing nature to produce spontaneously their crops of sugar, &c., &c.

During my stay at Realajo, a vessel arrived there for the purpose of procuring a cargo of sugar to take back to California, but not a pound could be obtained. The natives never think of "laying up for a rainy day," so the vessel returned with a cargo of limes, cigars, &c. Cigars of very superior quality were sold at that time for only $4 per 1,000, but it required considerable persuasion to induce the natives to make up a sufficient supply. Horses could be bought or hired at a very low rate, the owners caring more for the gaudily ornamented saddle and bridle, than for the fine animals they embellished. I was offered a sprightly, fine appearing horse for twenty-five dollars.

Poultry was abundant. Turtles were caught in large numbers along the sea-shore; the eggs were eaten raw by the natives with much gusto, but to me they tasted like castor oil.

Central America, settled by New Englanders, would become an important country, and yet there would be danger of even the enterprising Yankees becoming enervated by the warm climate.

On Friday, December 13th, we anchored in the beautiful bay of San Francisco, after a pleasant voyage. I was much surprised (although I had anticipated great and important changes,) at the wonderful progress that had been made in the improvements throughout the whole city during my absence. Streets widened and planked, elegant buildings erected, fine, substantial and commodious wharves, everything in fact wearing an aspect of comfort and prosperity.

On Friday, December 20th, I took passage on board the pretty little stern-wheel steamer, Jenny Lind, bound for Nicholaus. A marked difference was observable now from when I first started for the mines. Then the roads were scarcely perceptible; no accommodations by the wayside, and the disappointments and hardships of a pioneer's life, were cruel and severe. But it gives me pleasure to record, that the hardest part of my life in California had passed by; that I can now give some of the sunshine of a miner's life, and let the shadows be classed among the "things that were."

The passengers on board the steamer were social and agreeable; and after a fine supper, we puffed our Havanas, and kept up a jovial and interesting conversation until the "small hours" of morning admonished us to retire to the comfortable berths provided for us.

Saturday, December 21st. After breakfast we promenaded the upper decks, and contrasted our present mode of traveling and its attendant comfort, with that of a year previous. But look! the bell of the engineer is sounded, the steam is let off, the wheels cease revolving, a plank is pushed out, a passenger steps ashore—we have reached the *great town* of Nicholaus. The "good little Jenny" proceeded on her way, and I marched off to the St. Charles Hotel, which was conducted by my friend W——, with whom I had been connected in a similar business in San Francisco. Of course mutual congratulations were exchanged and the best room in the house was placed at my disposal, and that night for the first time in many months, I slept on a bed!

The streams and marshes contiguous to Nicholaus, were frequented by thousands and thousands of ducks and geese, and friend W—— expressed a wish to procure some of them for his Christmas dinner. Major A——, *formerly of the New York militia*, had boasted of being an excellent shot, and solicited my company on a gunning expedition, feeling sure that he could kill as many wild fowls as would answer for several dinners.

So W—— provided me with a double barrelled gun and plenty of ammunition, and on Tuesday, December 24th, the two sportsmen jumped into friend W——'s wagon, and away we went over the prairie, until we came to a stream, beyond which were the coveted objects of our ride; in plunged our swift chargers, but, as ill-luck would have it, the traces snapped asunder, and we were compelled to jump into the stream, and assist in getting out the wagon.

We waived a true military salute to W—— as he whipped up his horses, and left for the hotel; and away we marched until the major ordered a halt! "hold still, keep quiet, softly; you take to the right of that creek, and I will head them off."

Now, I had about as much experience in duck and goose shooting, as I have in harpooning a whale, but I obeyed orders; observing hundreds and hundreds of wild game flying around and above me, but like a brave warrior, I reserved my fire until I could rake several at a single shot. But hark! I hear the gallant major firing--bang, bang, away flew the geese and ducks; then they would alight at a little distance. But this was too much for my patience, it would not do for Major A—— to kill all the birds; so I concluded I would fire at the first bird that offered a good chance, without waiting to *mow them down;* but see there what a fine shot—a beautiful duck lazily swimming in the creek just beyond me. I raised my gun, took deliberate aim— and fired! I shot him, but just as I reached over the bank to secure my prize, up he flew—he was a diver!

Bang, bang, bang, the Major was sending forth a perfect "*feu de joie,*" certainly he must be bagging the game fast. I could see his tall slender form away over the marsh: now stooping, then erect, again cautiously approaching the now frightened birds; and here I had only fired once, and that a dead shot; but softly, look! is not that a crane to the left of me? I threw myself upon the ground, crawled like an Indian or an experienced hunter, slowly and cautiously, until I came within gunshot; then raised my double-barrelled gun, aimed, and fired! I looked up,—I saw the crane still standing. I felt sure I had killed it, although I scarcely remember whether I involuntarily closed my eyes, or that the heavy charge in the gun "kicked;" at any rate up I sprang, (I could see the Major standing off watching me,) ran to my prize, and what think you I shot at? The skull of a horse that had bleached in the sun! (The reader must know I am short sighted.)

Thus far I had fired two shots, and hit—the wind. The Major had fired at least a dozen rounds, how many he had killed I could not yet learn, but I supposed he had secured several plump birds for the dinner. "Look out! there's your chance, take gook aim at that flock of birds!" The Major was giving command. On they came. I raised my gun, fired at random, (satisfied it was unnecessary to take aim,) and killed—none!

By this time that excellent marksman (at least he boasted that he was,) and chief officer of the day—the Major—approached me, and inquired:

"How many did you shoot?"

"Not one," I replied. "How many did you bag Major?"

"Why, the powder is good for nothing—it has no strength; for although I made the feathers fly every time I fired, not one bird fell."

This was too much for my risibles. I roared out with laughter, but still the Major declared "that if the powder had been good, he would have brought down lots of game."

The day was nearly spent, and we had no birds secured for dinner. We sat down upon the green grass by a small stream, coursing along as quietly as the numerous ducks that were alighting and swimming near us, and I succeeded in getting my friend to admit that he and I were no marksmen. "But," said he, "it will not do to return without any game; we must make another trial, and if we fail, the powder must bear the blame.

We examined our guns—all right. Started off together, and came back to the creek without a single bird; and so we gave up in despair, and surrendered with as good grace as possible. Just as the sun was sinking behind the lofty range of mountains, just then two *experienced* hunters might have been seen entering the great city of Nicholaus, with excellent guns and ammunition thrown across their shoulders, but not a bird dangling from their persons.

On nearing the hotel we saw suspended from the balcony a string of birds, and we suspected our kind host had little confidence in our success. We reached the hotel; " here they come," saluted us, and when they learned the result, the very walls re-echoed with peals of laughter. The Major insisted that the good-for-nothing powder was damp, that although it made the feathers fly, it was not strong enough to carry shot.

We had to submit to any amount of quizzing, and the landlord remarked, " it occurred to me that possibly you might be unsuccessful, so I purchased a lot of birds to make sure of a supply for Christmas."

December 25th. Our Christmas dinner passed off pleasantly, the tables were arranged with a nicety worthy of a steamboat entertainment. Of course, our unsuccessful gunning expedition served as a fund of merriment to all who had the pleasure of dining at the St. Charles.

That night, I announced my determination of leaving

for the mines, for I was fearful my present luxurious style of living, would unfit me for the rough life of a miner. The Major and an old gentleman present expressed a willingness to accompany me, so we fixed upon the next day for starting.

CHAPTER XVII.

OFF FOR THE MINES—INCIDENTS ALONG THE ROAD—ARRIVAL AT GRASS VALLEY—THE DIGGER INDIANS—DISCOVERY OF GOLD-BEARING QUARTZ, &c., &c.

Thursday, December 26th, 1851. "Come old gentleman, 'tis time we were off." "Why, the wagon must be greased, the oxen haven't fed, and I think you young men had better lend a hand, than stand around giving orders."

Now, so far as I was concerned, I objected to the slow travel of an ox team, and the more the old man worried about his sleek, but lazy "critters," the less disposed his "fast nags" appeared to be yoked to a wagon. I had "seen the elephant," to use a California expression, but my "*compagnons de voyage*" had never been to the mines; and to hear them talk! They intended to introduce new customs among the miners, and they were going to live like gentlemen should. However, I must give the Major the credit of carrying out his intentions of living comfortably. At last "all were aboard," the long lash of the whip was applied to the oxen, and off they—walked! My acquaintances were supplied with an abundance of cooking utensils, bedding, et cetera, which were carefully packed in the covered wagon. I had very little baggage, intending to purchase where I located whatever mining and cooking utensils I might require; for I knew that the country was more thickly settled, and the opportunities for purchasing the comforts of life much greater, than when I made my first trip to the mines.

" Our "slow but sure line" was so wearisome to me, that I gladly took the whip, at the request of the owner, to have my turn at driving. I do not remember ever before having had the honor of driving a "coach and two," so I applied the lash, hallooed gee-woah-gee, until I frightened the heretofore gentle beasts, and off they trotted, making excellent time, and I do not know where my "lively team' would have brought up, had not the owner ran to my aid, ordered a halt, and declined my services in future as driver. Sometimes we walked, then rode, and occasionally halted to rest in the shade; for we could easily overtake the team, and I felt half inclined to travel on alone.

We expected to reach Finley's Ranch before dusk, but the "blooded stock" took their own time, and the owner of them was so accustomed to that mode of traveling, that he was as composed as a philosopher, by which name I shall hereafter designate him. We were just in sight of the ranch, and congratulated ourselves on our good fortune, when I looked ahead, and saw the philosopher applying the lash much more vigorously than even I had done; and I asked the major what could be the matter? We ran up, and found the wagon had stalled; the wheels were sunk to the hubs in the mud, and the poor oxen were striving their best to pull ahead; but snap, crack went the traces, off scampered the oxen, leaving the wagon in the mud. However, there was no use fretting about our ill-luck; for my part, I enjoyed the sport, but the temper of the philosopher was sorely tried. The best we could do was to drive the oxen into the corral, and let the wagon and cargo remain on the road.

Friday, December 27th. Arose early in the morning, settled bill at the tavern, looked up the oxen, repaired the damage to the wagon and gearing, and started off again in fine humor, the philosopher alternately singing and whistling, pronounced the road in "an awful condition"—"hard upon his stock." At night we stopped at "the round tent," which happened to be a square boarded house. I did not particularly admire the location, the landlord, or his accommodations.

Saturday, December 28th. "Hitched up" our fast team about 4 P. M., and started forward. The road was very rough, and the slow motion of our team suited very well now. Reached the "Zinc House," delightfully situated near never-failing streams; and while we washed our faces and enjoyed a rest in the welcome shade, our breakfast was prepared, and when the word was given, we lost no time in doing ample justice to the excellent repast mine host had spread before us. Bidding the landlord the "top of the morning," we followed after our patient and sure-footed oxen, and reached "Rough and Ready" during the afternoon; took a bird's eye view of the rough, but not ready looking place, and proceeded on until night overtook us, when we halted at the "Madison House," a rough, ill-shaped log hut, the meanest public house on the road.

Sunday, December 29th. The weather continued clear and pleasant, and it always appeared to me, that everything in nature assumed a more lovely and cheerful appearance on the Sabbath than on any other day of the week. I regretted that my peculiar life compelled me to travel on this day, which all are commanded to keep holy; but at that early period in the history of California, particularly at the mines, very few had opportunities of properly observing the Sabbath. We reached Grass Valley, Nevada Co., during the morning, and here I remained for many months, until, in fact, I bade a farewell—a long farewell to the Golden State.

Wednesday, January 1st, 1851. Here commences another year. I had been so many months in California that I became familiar with the hard life of a miner, and as I now lived much more comfortably than I had been previously accustomed to, I felt satisfied and contented.

The Major, the philosopher and myself worked on our own account. I still adhered to my determination not to join in partnership with any one, thus to avoid disputes and difficulties.

There were several encampments around here of native Indians, (the Digger tribe;) and one day, when working alone, some distance from my cabin, I was *honored* with a visit from several squaws, nearly every one of whom had a " papoose" strapped to her back. They were out hunting and digging wild onions and tender roots, which grew there; and they laughed heartily at my incessant digging and washing dirt, and signified that Indian no work, but " American much work, ugh," Their faces were besmeared with tar, which I was informed indicated the decease of a friend or relative.

Whilst I enjoyed a laugh at their expense, they were equally merry at the appearance I presented, so we were all pleased. Finally they went off, and I could hear them laughing at the idea of a man working and earning his support " by the sweat of his brow."

During this month, I paid occasional visits to Nevada

and Rough and Ready, each distant about four miles from Grass Valley. Nevada improved rapidly, and I could hardly recognize the place where I had lived and enjoyed the friendship of many choice spirits. Rough and Ready improved slowly, as her mines were not considered very "rich."

Thursday, January 30th. Five or six young men and myself agreed to take a short walk through the woods, ostensibly for "prospecting," but in reality to visit "Capt." Wemah's Indian camp. Our "prospecting amounted to the figure 0," but our visit to the Indians was interesting and highly gratifying. Their encampment was located in a lovely valley, through which ran a never-failing stream. Their council house was in the centre of the camp; around it were the wigwams, constructed of bark, each having a hole in the centre of the roof, through which issued the smoke from the fire beneath.

The entrance to their *palatial mansions* was an aperture just large enough to admit one person at a time in a stooping posture. On a large rock I noticed several squaws—quite pretty and of fine figure, nearly nude, pounding acorns, out of which they make soup and *bread*.

The *ladies* were courteous and affable, and were pleased with our visit, but apparently surprised at receiving so much attention from us. When the acorns are fully ripe, the squaws saunter forth, collect immense quantities, place them in their storehouse, and when needed, pound them to a coarse powder, which they prepare in a proper manner for the lazy chiefs.

The chiefs and braves never work, but spend their time in hunting and manufacturing ornaments. Whenever the squaws go out after roots and vegetables they are always accompanied by a brave, as a "guard of honor." I often wished that I could converse with them. The majority of the Indians about Grass Valley were friendly to the "whites;" others were disposed for war—war to extermination.

February, 1851. Directly opposite to my cabin was a hill seldom visited, except by an occasional miner in search of fire wood. By the merest chance gold-bearing quartz was discovered upon its summit. The report flew rapidly, and out of that discovery grew the important quartz mining, which revived the prospects of Grass Valley, and turned the attention of hundreds to quartz digging.

The hill was appropriately named Gold hill. Laws were established regulating the amount of feet each man could hold and work. A recorder was elected, and the hill was soon alive with men digging deep down in search of the quartz ledge—some of course were more fortunate than others. I have seen large quantities of rich specimens of quartz, thoroughly injected with bright, sparkling gold.

The plan of working was, first to dig up and cast away the surface dirt, and then a "well-like hole" was commenced, a windlass erected, a rope and bucket brought into requisition, and down, down, sometimes to the depth of forty and fifty feet, men would dig in search of a ledge, and if found, they would carefully break up the rock, carry it to their cabins, pound up the stone, and pocket the gold.

Saturday, February 22. I removed to Centerville, the main portion of Grass Valley, and rented a log cabin— one room, four dollars a month. My bedstead was constructed of poles and shingles, on the top of which I threw pine twigs, and then spread my blanket, and on this bed I slept for many a night as soundly and comfortably as I had ever done in my life.

Our town was fast improving; well furnished stores were established, hotels that offered comfortable quarters for travelers, a saw-mill was in active operation, and there were unmistakable evidences of growing wealth and prosperity. Among our inhabitants were some respectable women, and many intelligent and enterprising men. Every one felt, or ought to have felt, satisfied and good humored with himself and all around him.

CHAPTER XVIII.

GRASS VALLEY, NEVADA COUNTY—QUARTZ MINING—SPECULATORS—RAVINE MINING—WILD ANIMALS—THE WEATHER, &c., &c.

Wednesday, March 12th, 1851. A meeting of all who felt interested was held in my cabin, for the purpose of making laws for the government of a Hill, of which a party of friends had taken possession a day or two previously. As usual at all public meetings, the resolutions first offered were unanimously adopted. The Hill was named Cardinal, and myself elected Recorder. My duty was to record the name of every claim holder, for which I received one dollar each, and fifty cents for a transfer. A large number of claims were recorded, and had the Hill proved as rich in auriferous deposits as its opposite neighbor, Gold Hill, I should have realized many hundred dollars by simply writing down names in a book.

I was often amused by parties from San Francisco, calling on me as the "executive officer" of Cardinal Hill, to locate claims for them; they supposing that by virtue of my office, I could tell at a glance where the gold was secreted. Each claim-holder was entitled to 30 by 60 feet of ground, divided off by stakes driven into the four corners of the lot, with one in the centre, designating the number of the lot. This was its lock and key, for the miners respected the laws enacted by their own fraternity. Whilst I lived there, Cardinal Hill was not considered the best place to invest money and labor, although there were certain indications of the existence of gold.

The reports from Gold Hill were exceedingly encouraging, and unprincipled speculators visited our locality to purchase quartz specimens, took them to other places, and by false representations, would sometimes succeed in selling mining lots. Others, I was informed, would send specimens to the eastern cities, form companies, sell stock, pocket the proceeds of their iniquity, and that ended their connection with their reputed "rich diggings."

Dishonest tricks very rarely could be played off upon real bona-fide miners. But I heard of a game successfully practised upon new comers, which resulted, however, entirely different from what was intended or desired.— Two men had been working their claim along side of a ravine for some time without the slightest prospect of success, and they conceived the idea of "making it pay" the first opportunity that presented. Some men who had just arrived at the mines, happening to pass this claim, asked the usual questions about mines and mining, and were answered that the best plan was to purchase a claim, and then they could commence work at once, for time was money in California. They requested the strangers to call in the morning to have a further talk. After they left, the chaps put about an ounce of gold dust into the bottom of the pit they were digging, and when the next day came round, and with it the strangers, the men who knew there was no gold to be found but what they had placed there, spoke of their claim as yielding rich returns, and as an evidence of it they would pan out *just* a shovel full of dirt, and they might judge for themselves. The result surprised and excited the strangers; they bought the claim for two hundred dollars, threw off their coats, rolled up their sleeves, and went to work, encouraged by bright anticipations and joyful hopes; but as often as they panned out, so often were they doomed to disappointment, until at last they suspected they "were sold;" but agreed to work on and dig deeper. After working nearly a week longer, the earth assumed a different color; they panned out once more, and to their infinite joy, found they had "struck a rich vein," and after all, made considerable gain upon their purchase, and the laugh was turned on the other side.

A friend left in my care a large iron mortar, about three feet high, which I found very useful, as it assisted me materially in "pocketing" the gold. I had the mortar placed in a solid block of wood, and a pole attached to the handle of the pestle, which answered as an excellent lever. Then I bought up all the gold-bearing quartz I could procure, and now pounded my rocks with comparative ease

to a coarse powder. At evening I would pan this out
in a tub nearly filled with water, and occasionally made
considerable profit by my speculations. But I too had
my losses. On one occasion I purchased two cart-loads
of stone, for which I paid one hundred and twenty-five
dollars. I was some time engaged in pounding up this
lot, and even before I had finished, I knew it was a
losing bargain; but I continued to purchase any lots
that were offered, and sometimes the yield was immense. A great many men preferred the river and the
dry diggings. Mining implements had undergone a vast
improvement since the days of my first experience in mining. Then we used a rocker or cradle; now the "long-tom" was introduced, by which twenty times as much dirt
could be washed out. A long-tom is a trough about sixteen feet long, with a perforated sheet of iron inserted at
one end; water is let on, and dirt thrown in, which it
is only necessary to stir up and throw out the stones.
It was a strange sight to see a hundred men working in
pits, some digging, some throwing up the mud and stones,
others shoveling it into the box, and others again stirring
up the mass and throwing out the rocks. The noise was
so great that one could scarcely hear any thing beside the
incessant rattle, rattle, rattle. Men worked faithfully,
constantly and expeditiously. At night, around the place
where hundreds had been working, splashing and rattling

away during the day, all was still and quiet. Nothing could be heard but the harsh unpleasant howl of the many "kiota," a species of prairie wolf, that always swarmed around the village at night in search of food. These dog-shaped animals were as cowardly as they were treacherous; one person could frighten off a drove of them, and I frequently heard the report of a gun fired off among them. The kiotas burrow after dead bodies like the hyena, and they congregate at night wherever they can find cast-off meat, carrion, &c.

For a novelty we had an occasional sprinkling of snow during the last three days of March; but when April made its bow, the snow vanished. No ice formed during the past winter, and the citizens of San Francisco and Sacramento were sadly put to it for that luxury, until some shrewd, enterprising men brought snow from the mountains, and furnished them with it at almost fabulous prices. I believe the first ice that was brought to California was from Sitka, a Russian possession, in the good old ship Flavius, the same vessel I have so often referred to— the same in which I had sailed to California.

CHAPTER XIX.
GRASS VALLEY—NEVADA COUNTY—A GRAND CONCERT—MINES AND MINING.

April, 1851. I find many pleasing reminiscences connected with my residence in Grass Valley, but none that afforded me greater pleasure than the frequent re-unions with several of my acquaintances after the onerous duties of the day were over. We met at one or the other's cabin, and sang the songs that were familiar to us prior to our residence in California.

The attractive power of music was strikingly exemplified in the large number of persons who congregated around us. The old-fashioned, simple plaintive tunes, such as "Auld Lang Syne," " Good-bye," " Coming thro' the Rye," " John Anderson," &c., &c., were always called for, and doubtless, these songs would bring to mind other days, other scenes, and other friends. Even the most boisterous, the most careless and indifferent, would stop to listen to these, (I am sorry to say, now unfashionable songs,) and occasionally wipe away an unbidden tear.

Our singing created a strong friendship among the half dozen young men who thus often met together, and as the majority of us performed upon some musical instrument, to the possession of this accomplishment, I attribute in a great measure, the extensive and valued acquaintance I enjoyed in California.

One evening, when singing merrily, thus dispelling gloom and sadness, and forgetful of any deprivation we may have labored under, some one proposed giving a a concert for the benefit of the landlord of the " Magnolia," which met the approval of all, and we very soon made out a famous programme. As there was no printing office in our midst, one of the party being a good penman, wrote out several programmes on sheets of paper. We posted them on the trees, houses and fences, and had the satisfaction of knowing that the promised concert gave rise to considerable excitement. Those not in the secret inquired, " Who are they ?" We preserved our incognito. Our bills were headed " Grand Vocal and Instrumental Concert by the Grass Valley Minstrels. Cards of admission only 50 cents. The choicest gems from the most popular operas will be performed, and the most attractive Ethiopian songs will be introduced, delineating high life among the Southern Negroes." We issued complimentary tickets to every female living in and around our village. Our troupe consisted of Mr. C. and brother, professional musicians ; Dr. D., of Maine ; Dr. C., of New Orleans ; Mr. H., formerly a head clerk in a large banking house; Mr. T., a dentist, formerly from Boston, and myself. Our ushers were gentlemen who had once counted thousands as their own. Each one connected with the affair anticipated fine sport, and at the same time determined to impart his joyful feelings to the audience. On Monday evening, April 7th, the grand concert took place. Long before the curtain rose the house was crowded. The ushers, with their kids and fancy neck-ties, were busy showing the eager crowd seats, and when the bell sounded for the performers to make their bow to the audience, those of us who had never yet appeared "upon any stage," began to feel a "little queer," when the *Director* called out—" Come, gentlemen, march in." Now it fell to my lot to lead the way, and about the third step I tripped and fell, two or three at my back tumbled over me, and this little incident, not set down in the bills, " brought down the house." Our faces were painted the color of *Mason's challenge blacking*, and well for me they were, or my cheeks would have exhibited a scarlet blush. The leader tapped—the overture commenced—the applause was great; but I hardly know whether it was called forth by our *fine* music, or the grotesque appearance we presented.

The next piece was a solo, performed by myself on the flute. The third piece was a song, with full *orchestral* accompaniments. This was delightfully received. The *appreciative* audience were in extacies; but when the commedians were introduced, the applause was terrific. I began to weary of the exhibition we were making of ourselves, and certainly did not shed tears when the first part was concluded and we adjourned to our private room.— The landlord was in the best humor; our every want was anticipated; he well knew that a couple of hundred dollars would soon be handed to him. But hark! the bell rings. The leader pronounced the instruments in tune. Forward! The curtain rose—the audience applauded. We took our seats, but somehow or other our insruments accorded better in the "green room" than on the stage; but we played away, sang and talked nonsense to the infinite amusement of the crowd, who were wondering "who those chaps were." The last piece was soon to be played. The leader gave the signal. The violin shrieked; the guitar was out of tune; the hideous bones rattled; the abominable triangle gave forth about as sweet music as a tin-pan, and the flute chimed in. We played away ; the audience were charmed; the musicians "got off the track"— one played "Yankee Doodle," another "Hail Columbia," and another, "Oft in the stilly night"—but it mattered not, "the steam was up." We fiddled away until the curtain dropped. The concert was over, and we sat down to enjoy rest and a capital supper the landlord had prepared for us. Speeches were made. We separated in the best humor with each other and our evening's performance. We sought our cots and slept as soundly as our instruments did lying in the chimney corner. The concert was long talked of. We had numerous invitations to visit neighboring districts; but it was the first and last concert the Grass Valley Minstrels ever gave.

Claims were still in demand on Cardinal Hill; but I sold out my interest in claim No. 4, making a good bargain, and ceased working there, satisfied with the profits derived from the office of Recorder.

Another hill was seized by a party of miners, and the name of Massachusetts Hill was given to it. I had a claim there also; but as the ledge of quartz ran very deep, I knew it would be useless for me to hold it, so I sold out at an advance. However, the parties who purchased of me succeeded in getting out about three thousand dollars' worth of gold.

But there was no hill yet discovered "so rich" as the appropriately named, Gold Hill. Quartz mills were rapidly put up, and miners could have their rock crushed for a certain sum, or dispose of it to other parties. The successful quartz mining in our valley brought many strangers amongst us. But ravine mining was not neglected. Some of my acquaintances had valuable claims, and none doubted that Grass Valley would continue to prosper and become a prominent place, and I will hereafter describe the village, the county, the inhabitants, and many "little incidents" that came under my observation.

CHAPTER XX.
POLITICAL SENTIMENTS—A DEMONSTRATION—GRASS VALLEY—HER MAGISTRATES.

Saturday, April 12th, 1851. At this period the Whig and Democratic parties were pitted against each other. Friends of either party brought with them to California their old feelings of devotion and enthusiasm for their favorite candidates and principles, or hatred and prejudice against their opponents. But the skill of an astrologer was not requisite to divine which of the two parties would ultimately succeed. I am free to confess that I was an active "Henry Clay Whig," but my exertions in behalf of that once-powerful party amounted to nothing, for our party invariably came off "second best." But "*nihil desperandum*" was our watchword.

An election for county officers was soon to take place, and for the office of sheriff there were several candidates who offered their services for their "country's good." Among them was an illiterate, conceited, and unpopular representative of "mein faderland," who nominated himself as a candidate for the *high office* of sheriff of Grass Valley township. He contended that his invaluable services in the Texan war of independence entitled him to an election, and yet his name was unknown to those real

Texas rangers who lived among us; and his own countrymen (many of whom I knew and esteemed highly) disliked him. One thing the would-be warrior possessed, and that was a valuable quartz claim. He was desirous that a "demonstration" should be made in his behalf. A party of lively fellows, always ready for sport, encouraged the idea. They procured the hotel gong, and sounded it so loud that it could be heard above the bells that were ringing; and when they fired off guns and pistols, no wonder that a large crowd collected and enquired— "what's up now?" Nine cheers for the Texas warrior were given with a will. Mein Herr mounted the stump, essayed to define his principles, but at almost every word he was greeted with "hip, hip, hurrah!" It was not surprising that he appeared delighted to see around him so many friends who could scarcely restrain their cordial sympathetic feelings!

He was followed by a Nevada lawyer—hired for the occasion—who praised the candidate to the skies. "For," said he, "if San Francisco has her brave Jack Hays for sheriff, if Sacramento has her gallant Ben McCullough, why cannot Grass Valley have her intrepid, bold, chivalric Texan warrior for sheriff, especially as he is the owner of such a fine grey horse!" "Bravo, good, one hundred yells;" the pistols banged away, the bells rang, and the gong sent forth most unearthly sounds.

The volunteer candidate was in the happiest humor— who could doubt his election? He at once sprang to the stump, silence was ordered, (a few persons knew what was in the wind) and invited all his friends to a grand treat at the "Beatty House." A procession was formed, headed by Mein Herr and his Nevada orator, and away they marched for the hotel, and toasted and drank, to the election of the Texas warrior, until the night was far spent.

That "demonstration" cost the volunteer candidate upwards of two hundred dollars. The election came off a few days subsequently, and the warrior received two votes! Alas! the uncertainty of politics!

Main street was the Broadway of Grass Valley. It was wide, and flanked on either side by comfortable weather-boarded houses. Among them were the principal hotels, saloons and stores, and through it led the direct road to Nevada and Rough and Ready. But Mill street, so named in consequence of the quartz mills located thereon, was likewise an important street, and a delightful walk led through it to the Indian camp. I do not know that I ever felt more comfortably than when promenading through that street, observing the miners hard at work, the improvements going on, and enjoying the pure and delicious mountain air.

My acquaintance with the population was extensive, and among them were persons of high social worth, intellectual acquirements, and gentlemanly deportment. The chief magistrate of the township was Judge S——, formerly of Boston. He was a man of "infinite jest and exquisite fancy." Certainly the best informed lawyer in the village, and before whom most of the "law cases" were tried. I was often amused at the Judge, to see him living in his old log cabin, preparing with his own hands the substantials for the inner man, sleeping in an almost dilapidated bed; puffing away at his favorite meerschaum, and entering into fellowship with his numerous acquaintances. No wonder he was always elected to office by a large majority over his competitors. I shall not soon forget the free, happy, delightful hours we spent together. May he long live to enjoy the comforts and pleasures of life.

Magistrate No. 2 was formerly of Missouri. He was an exceedingly clever and hospitable man, but totally unqualified for the office to which he was elected by a flattering majority. Perhaps he may remember the merry times we had; perhaps he has not forgotten the marriage of his daughter. How we serenaded him; how our cheers and congratulations re-echoed through the woods, and how he, in pleasurable excitement, headed a large party of friends, and marched to the Beatty House, "where we had a good time all around." How he mounted the table—clad only in his night garment—and thanked his friends and neighbors for this "unexpected mark of esteem for himself individually, and for their congratulations upon the happy marriage of his daughter."

Justice No. 3 was Mr. R——, also of Missouri. He was popular as a man, but totally incapacitated for the office to which he was elected by a handsome majority. I have felt very much for poor R—— when the shrewd, fun-provoking lawyers would call upon "his honor" to explain to the jury the facts of the case, but his honor would sit still, run his fingers through his hair, and say nothing.

CHAPTER XXI.

SUNDAY AT THE MINES—ADVICE TO PARENTS—A LECTURE—SKETCH OF SOME OF THE INHABITANTS, &c.

Sunday, April 27th. As yet no religious associations had been organized in Grass Valley; but many who had not forgotten their earlier training, met together on Sabbath evenings, and sang the familiar hymns of "days of yore." The American miners generally abstained from secular work; they donned their best clothing, read their Bible, looked over their correspondence, and visited acquaintances, or enjoyed a walk around the beautifully located village.

In this connection, let me advance the suggestion to parents to " train up their children in the way they should go." Let me urge upon them to repeat, not only "Our Father who art in heaven," but those heartfelt, simple hymns, which touch the feelings, and make a lasting impression on the heart. No parent knows what will be the future of a child; no parent knows where a favorite child may roam, or in what clime he may dwell; but if a mother has taught that child to kneel by her side, and pray to God to protect not only himself, but each member of his family, that prayer is never forgotten—that mother's watchfulness is never obliterated from the mind. At some time or other that parental solicitude is remembered, and protects the wanderer. Many who were residing in California, found in their trials great comfort in repeating the prayers of childhood, and experienced a peculiar delight in singing the hymns which they had sung at home in the Sabbath School.

We were occasionally favored with a lecture by some of the residents, many of whom were men of talent and education.

Mr. John A. C——, formerly of New York, delivered an able and interesting lecture on the evils of intemperance. He did not villify and traduce the unfortunate victim of alcoholic stimulants, but he merely pictured, in glowing words and manner, the horrible results of the too free use of that vile stuff which men sometimes "put in their mouths to steal away their brains." The principal portion of his auditory were miners, and because he spoke charitably and sympathetically of the poor inebriate, they paid him the most marked attention. I shall have occasion to speak of Mr. C—— hereafter.

Among the physicians resident here, with whom I was most intimate, were Dr. C——, formerly of Ohio; Dr. S.——, from Mississippi, and Dr. ——, from St. Louis.

Dr. C—— was very popular; associated with the people, had an extensive practice, and for a while acted as postmaster. I remember on one occasion the Dr. was called to visit a patient at some distance from the village, and he solicited me to act as postmaster during his absence. The mail from the Eastern States was daily expected, and hundreds of men were anxiously waiting the arrival of the stage. Towards the close of the day the rumbling of the wheels was heard—the stage was seen descending the hill—snap, snap, cracked the whip—woa, woa, woa,—the horses were resting in front of the post-office. I seized the package marked Grass Valley, and soon announced to the eager crowd that the mail from the east had arrived; and to facilitate the distribution, and prevent any unnecessary delay, I would read out the names as they were placed in the package; of course, this announcement gave great satisfaction, and the new postmaster was complimented; but my responsibilities ended that night. So I sang out—A. J. Compton—"That's mine, sir;" Wm. Elder—"Mine, sir;" and so I kept on until I distributed every letter in the bag; but not one letter did I find directed to myself.

Doctor No. 2, was friend S———, from Mississippi, who graduated at the same college with myself—that is nowhere! S——— had some practice, but was more successful in speculating in real estate. The Dr. showed me a daguerreotype of himself he was about to send to his family, and for the occasion he divested himself of his coat and vest, put a wash-pan under his arm, laid a pick and shovel at his feet—thus giving the impression that he was earning his living by hard work.

The other M. D., whose name I have forgotten, I remember as a gentleman of fine personal appearance and courteous manners, and with whom every one must have been pleased.

Of the merchants, I class Capt. C———, formerly of Brooklyn, No. 1. The captain had left a home in which he enjoyed all the comforts and luxuries of life;—he had emigrated to California for what? To satify an uncontrollable desire for roaming in search of novelty. The captain had left a happy home, where dwelt an affectionate wife and favorite daughter, but he must forsake all, and at an advanced time of life, seek the wilds of California, and engage in the perplexing duties of a merchant's life. Frequently I partook of the captain's hospitality, and often before daylight appeared, has he urged me "to come over and take breakfast with him." Many, many happy hours I have spent in his society, and if wishes can do any good, I here tender him ten thousand for his safe return home, and his permanent settlement there in peace and happiness.

P——, from New York, commenced in a small way, but by close attention to business, built up a considerable trade.

E—— was also from New York. Born in Scotland, raised in New York, an orthodox Presbyterian, correct in his habits, generally esteemed, and did a fine business.

K—— and L—— were from Maine, easy, good natured fellows—not much experience in merchandising, but still had cheering prospects.

W—— was from Canada, an extensive traveler; well educated; did a flourishing business; minded his own affairs; small in stature, but tough as a Canadian pony.

While these brief sketches of the inhabitants may not interest all readers, still, there may be some who will find pleasure in reading of their friends and relatives "far off in California," and all may observe how strangely peopled California was; men from every state, bringing with them their peculiar notions and prejudices, and yet the influence of a few moral and intellectual gentlemen kept in check the turbulent spirit that needed only a spark to ignite it into a flame.

CHAPTER XXII.

GRASS VALLEY—NEVADA COUNTY—LOCAL MATTERS.

Thursday, May 1st, 1851. The weather at this time was charming; not a cloud in the sky above to obscure the effulgent sun; and when men went forth to work at early dawn, the delightful and invigorating atmosphere inspired all with the happiest feelings, and each man hoped that his claim would this day yield up its treasures so abundantly, as to permit him to look forward to a speedy return home. Home! what happy feelings thrill the inmost soul at the mention of that word.

Friday, May 2d. Our whig friends held their first meeting, for the purpose of appointing delegates to a county convention to be held at Nevada the ensuing day. The harmony and good feeling which prevailed was gratifying to the entire assemblage.

Professor S——, formerly of Ohio, delivered a lecture upon mining; it puzzled his audience to understand how a man could point out the best place to work, and yet not be enabled to find a profitable claim for himself!

The lawyers of our village, whom I knew intimately, were Judge ———, formerly of St. Louis. A gentleman reserved in his general deportment, but was much respected, and gracefully submitted to an "emigrant's life" in California.

Lawyer No. 2 was a clever, social, gentlemanly representative of Canada. His practice was considerable, and daily increasing.

Our town constable was one of those quiet, reserved men, who are liked, and still one can hardly tell why. He was elected to office by a large majority over his competitors. He informed me that his office fees averaged about one hundred dollars a week. The Legislature had not yet reduced the exorbitant fees demanded by judges, magistrates, jurors, and constables; and woe to the luckless wight who became entangled in the meshes of the law.

Sunday, May 4th. Mr. C—— delivered another lecture; the subject this time was "The evils resulting from Gambling." He acquitted himself admirably, but it was like the play entitled, "Love's Labor Lost." The general state of the society in our town was excellent. We had as yet no houses for religious worship; the town was not incorporated; each man was free to act as he thought proper; and yet we had no robberies, no murders, but every one appeared anxious to have our little village distinguished for its morality.

Wednesday, May 7th. The flowers in full bloom; away over the marshes, on the mountain top, as far as the eye could reach, could be seen beautiful flowers of the most gorgeous colors, and yet without perfume, save the violet, the sweetest of them all, which filled the air with its delightful fragrance. Often and often I sauntered out and gathered the prettiest to adorn my rude cabin.

There were a couple of bakers among us, but clever Johnny, from "swate Ireland," did the best business. My bill for bread averaged one dollar a week, and as the greater number of our citizens purchased their bread, Johnny accumulated a goodly amount of the "root of all evil." If my memory serves me aright, he had upwards of ten thousand dollars deposited in one of the banking houses of San Francisco. Johnny would once a week bake pies and cakes, which always sold readily at high prices; but most of his customers would have declined them at any price, had they been at their "homes in the East," as we used to say.

Claims were still called for on Cardinal Hill, and if ever I made money without much labor, it was in performing the duties of Recorder.

But if disputes arose concerning claims, the Recorder was supposed to be possessed of wondrous wisdom, and it was necessary to assume a magisterial air. I remember, on one occasion, a party of fellows took possession of a portion of Cardinal Hill, gave it a name, elected a Recorder, and pretended that their side was vastly the most profitable. Now came my turn to exercise the dignity and importance of my office; and as I was a man of peace, not disposed for "54.40 or fight," I began to think my office was not so comfortable as I had supposed. Cardinal Hill demanded her right, and called its chief officer to " go at once and dispossess the intruders."

Now, some things are much easier talked about than done; however, I bristled up courage, marched off for the residence of the executive officer of Wolf's Hill— as they called it—and soon made known who I was, and what I wanted. The man resembled that *tame bird* called the mastiff, and the war of words we kept up was loud enough to startle the Indians, whose camp was near by. I insisted that the entire hill belonged to the Cardinal company; and knowing their rights and claims, I demanded a surrender of our property! Why; my argument had about as much influence on the man, as the fly which occasionally lit upon his cranium. He declared his determination to hold on to that portion of the hill which his company claimed—that he had as much right to its possession as any body else. I was accompanied by one friend only, whose physical prowess was about equal to my own. Our opponent was surrounded by a dozen of his chums, each one of whom looked as though they had rather fight than say their prayers. And I, admiring the maxim, that " the better part of valor is discretion," considered it prudent to return to my friends, which I did, and received their congratulations and thanks for so boldly venturing alone on such a mission to such characters, although I failed to accomplish the object of my mission. Our party talked the matter over, and as there was a narrow ravine running through the hill, which may have answered as a dividing line, we let the matter rest, and thus ended a dispute which threatened disastrous consequences, and its peaceable termination relieved me of considerable anxiety and annoyance.

Sunday, May 10th. Delightful weather, and I enjoyed the day very pleasantly with numerous friends. But it was a strange mode of life: abstaining from all secular work, and no place of religious worship. It was a day when friends visited each other, talked over the scenes and occurrences of childhood, the transactions of life at maturity, the causes of emigration to California, and the prospects of the future. How many recollections arise in the mind of a wanderer in a distant land; how frequently we think of pleasures we enjoyed, and resolve, if ever we return, that we will do thus and so. What a delightful pleasure it is to hope. Hope! the sheet-anchor of an adventurer's life! Truly, every Californian can appreciate the "pleasures of hope;" and may every one of them realize their best wishes.

CHAPTER XXIII.

MY CABIN—A SERMON—A FIRE, ALMOST—MY PETS—AN ACQUAINTANCE, &c., &c.

Saturday, June 7th, 1851. I now lived in my own cabin, located on a gently rising hill, within sight of Centreville or Grass Valley, and very often was the only human being dwelling upon that mountain. But I became much attached to my shingle cabin. Many a night when the wind blew a perfect hurricane, when the lightning flashed most vividly, the thunder roared the loudest, and the rain poured down the fiercest—many a night did I sleep alone in that fragile cabin—no human being within the sound of my voice; and I loved that rude old hut and the very trees that sheltered it. Is it not strange how we can habituate ourselves to seeming inconveniences and deprivations? My cabin was constructed of poles and shingles; not a pane of glass about the premises; and the only light I enjoyed came in when I left open the door. The chimney was of an *elegant* style of architecture; but of a design, which, a Chinese only could describe. The floor of my mansion—oh, I am writing too hurriedly—the ground was covered with pine twigs, which answered very well until I pulled off my boots! My bedstead was of the latest French pattern in one particular, and that was its low posts; but it was remarkable for its durability; the thick shingles nailed across the untrimmed poles, never gave way. My table was of the plainest style, four round sticks, and about a dozen shingles composed that necessary article of furniture, and my cupboard was most admirable for stowing away provisions, only it lacked sides and a door! But I shall, in course of time, speak more particularly of the trees, my arbor, and grounds, for I possessed quite an estate, and no wonder strangers passing by inquired, "who lives there?"

The principal "diggings," Centreville ravine and Mud flat, classic names! were within sight of my new abode. The town was about a quarter of a mile distant, and the only inhabitants that favored me with their continual presence were snakes—bah! the hideous things haunt me now. A lonely owl, which perched itself on a lofty pine close by my cabin, every night honored me with a serenade, which was any thing but agreeable; and rats! why I had them by hundreds, and they were of the largest species. But my favorite pets were lizards! Every time I sat down to eat, they would crawl into my cabin to be fed with crumbs of bread. I can recollect when the intrusion of such pets would have quickly driven me from the table.

But I possessed a healthy location, pure water, delightful shade, privacy and quiet. Now, I sometimes wonder how I could muster courage to remain so long a time on that mountain alone. Depraved men occasionally passed through our valley, and again Indians, who were known to be hostile to the whites; but I never was attacked in going to my cabin at a late hour, even in the darkest night. Nor was I molested at any time, although I could easily have been robbed and murdered in my hut, the intruders escaping, and perhaps never being detected. Often and often have friends urged me "to move further down the hill;" but I loved my isolated residence, and continued its occupant until I left for the Atlantic states.

The prices of provisions and clothing were gradually falling, and miners could live much more economically than a few months previously. Then, there was little competition in trade; now, stores were established, which could have supplied many more inhabitants than were living in our beautiful valley.

Sunday, June 8th. Fine weather; spent the day very agreeably; in the afternoon listened to a sermon by Rev. Dr. H——, of the Episcopal church; very few attended; and it was the first and last discourse the doctor preached there. He did not like the idea of holding forth to empty benches. The larger portion of his audience had never before attended service as conducted by the Episcopalians, and I feared some of them were strangers to any religious exercises.

Monday, June 9th. The trees which flourished best in our neighborhood were the oak and pine; and at that time wood cost nothing; so every miner kept up a blazing fire; and well they did, for the nights were always cool, and during the winter months, when the rain poured down and thoroughly drenched their fragile cabins, these comfortable fires prevented a vast amount of sickness. I came near losing my *palatial* habitation on one occasion. I greatly feared that I should be overrun by the million of ants that were holding a mass convention near me, and I saw they had agreed "by acclamation" to take possession of my provisions "*sans ceremonie.*" So I threw hot ashes over the first battalion, and passed on to the city, hoping, upon my return, I would find that my enemy had "retreated." As I was returning, not dreaming of anything amiss, some friend sang out to me, "look ahead, your cabin is on fire." I hastened my steps, and soon discovered that the hot ashes had ignited the dried leaves lying around, and the flames were fast extending towards my cabin. I took things very calmly; reached for my long shovel, and pitched the burning leaves as far off as possible. Fortunately, they lodged upon a bank of clay, and thus I saved my hut, drove off the ants, and sitting down, partook of a frugal repast, grateful that I still possessed a shelter, humble though it was.

Among the miners, Thomas Y——, formerly of New

York, was my most intimate and valued acquaintance. We lived in adjoining cabins for a considerable time; we felt truly interested in each other's success and happiness, and enjoyed many a delightful walk and conversation, which, doubtless, we shall remember with pleasure as long as memory performs its office. My friend Y. knew my fondness for odd pets; so he shot in the wing, a large crow, brought it to me, and said, "there, now you have a pet." I found my "black bird" would not consent to be confined in the cabin, so I tied a rope to his leg, and fastened it to a log, where he strutted and cawed, cawed to his heart's content. He became so friendly that he would eat from my hands; but one day I missed him, and never knew whether some fellow stole him, or whether he gnawed the rope in twain, and "took leg bail."

The most hideous thing I saw in California was a horn-ed frog. I gave him a wide berth; but perhaps the tarantula which I once came near putting my hand upon, was even more disgusting. This poisonous reptile was honored by being pinioned to a post!

Those persons who were fond of gunning, had capital sport; game in abundance. Deer, bears, antelopes, rabbits, squirrels, ducks and geese, birds of nearly every kind; and those fond of angling met with great success, for the rivers and streams teemed with a variety of the choicest fish, although the Indians declared "the smoke-ships of the whites frightened off the finny tribe in the big waters."

CHAPTER XXIV.

GRASS VALLEY—MINES IN SUMMER AND WINTER—FIRE—A HERMIT—A FRIEND.

June 14th, 1851. The great difficulty which miners labored under at this time, was in procuring a sufficient supply of water to wash their " dirt." No water and ditch companies had yet been formed, and men who owned valuable claims, were compelled to exercise the patience of grandfather Job, in waiting until the rainy season came around. Most persons are doubtless aware that the climate of California is vastly different from that of any other state in the confederacy. During the summer months not a drop of water descends upon the parched ground, and those settlements destitute of never-failing streams, present a languishing aspect. But the winter months bring copious showers, and during this season everything assumes a cheerful appearance, and the miner's heart is gladdened.

The miners who possessed valuable claims, and yet had no water to "run their dirt" through the long-tom, generally remained and employed their time during the summer season in throwing up the dirt, which dried in the sun, and, of course, washed out more easily during the winter.

A ravine at this season of the year (June) presented a singular appearance. Here were deep holes dug, around them, heaps of dirt thrown up—over there a pile of stones and rocks exposed to the sun, which, a few months previously, had been buried deep within the earth, and perhaps had lain undisturbed for centuries. Near by were parts of washing machines which had done good service, but were now warped and cracked; and—look out!—walk cautiously, see that singularly worked hole, let us go down; there are the props which sustain the bank above; there are the various rooms, swept clean as a parlor floor, not a particle of gold can be found; the owners carefully followed the "lead," dug up and washed out the paying dirt, and burrowed under in that peculiar manner so as to save the expense of "throwing off top dirt." It was a system of mining called "kiotying," taken from the kiota, an animal that burrows under the ground.

Fire, fire, fire! the alarm was sounded—every inhabitant felt excited—run, men, run! All the houses were constructed of poles and shingles, lined with muslin or paper, and should the fire spread, good-bye to our village; we had no fire engines, and no water convenient. Fire! fire! Where? Down "Mill street." I saw the flames issuing from one of friend S——'s houses; fortunately, it stood

alone, and the evening was calm. The building was
consumed. The fire extended no farther, and the danger
was over.

The "vigilance committee" was in full sway in San
Francisco; many outlaws who were "spotted" left for
the mining districts, and although many dangerous looking fellows passed through our village, we were not disturbed by any of them. Our town was not incorporated,
and although a few selfish and designing men tried their
utmost to have it incorporated, still they were inglo-
riously defeated, and we continued in our old course, and
few, if any settlements in California could exhibit a more
moral and virtuous people. I found much to interest and
amuse me in my leisure hours in listening to the history
of some of the inhabitants. There was one known as the
hermit, who rarely communicated with any one; he was
looked upon as a selfish, morose, and unsocial being; he
wore a heavy moustache and whiskers, and yet there was an
air of refinement and a gentlemanly bearing about him,
which interested me exceedingly, and excited a desire to
learn something of his past history. Circumstances threw
us together, and we became quite intimate. I was his first
guest at his table. His cabin was constructed in the form
of a soldier's tent. You opened into his bed chamber;
everything neatly arranged; the ground covered with
fresh pine twigs, and the adjoining room was his kitchen,

7*

his store-room, &c., &c. There was his convenient mantel, and his serviceable fire-place; his chair with a table attached, upon which he ate his meals, stood in the centre of the room, and when we sat down to dine, everything was in excellent order, and we enjoyed ourselves exceedingly. We met often afterwards; for a short time we mined together, and during our walks through the delightfully shaded woods, I learned his history, which interested me so much, that I will endeavor to relate it, as nearly as I can recollect in his own words, feeling assured it will interest all. "At the expiration of the year 18--, I stood at my office door in Wall street, New York, worth fifty thousand dollars clear of the world. This amount I considered sufficient for my wants, and I had determined to retire from business; but just as I was about to leave the office, my partners urged me to continue one year longer, saying, that their business was increasing, and there was every probability of doubling that amount in twelve months. After reflecting a few moments, I yielded to their wishes. I continued as a bill and exchange broker twelve months longer, and at the expiration of that time, stood in front of the office worth not one cent!

"A financial crisis arose, it affected our house, and I went forth a poor, miserable and disappointed man. In the meanwhile, the beloved wife of my choice, died— an only child was left me. I placed the little babe in

charge of her mother's family, and started westward.
The California gold excitement broke out. I rushed to
the new El Dorado, and by working early and late, succeeded in accumulating several thousand dollars, which I
sent to my friends to be invested as a permanent fund for
the sole use of my little daughter. Then I breathed
freer. I was able to supply the wants of my little darling, and now I work on, work faithfully to accumulate
sufficient to visit her, to take her under my own care, and
teach her the religion of Christ!"

Among my numerous acquaintances, I shall ever remember another with whom I was most intimate, the most
familiar friend he had outside of his own family; but he is
now sleeping his last sleep beneath the cold clods of the
valley. The choicest flowers, planted by the hand of affection, are blooming, doubtless, over his grave. He was
a man of fine classical attainments; had traveled over
many lands, and his colloquial powers were of the highest
order. At his southern home, he was universally beloved, and had occupied offices of trust and honor. His description of his travels through Europe, I remember with
profit and pleasure. Only one incident I will mention.
He was about entering Madame Tussaud's wax-figure exhibition in London, and seeing, as he supposed, Madame
Tussaud, sitting in the hall, wearing a pleasant smile, he
bowed politely, and passed on; but observing some gen-

tlemen laughing, he asked the cause of their mirth, as their attention seemed directed to him. They answered—" You have been bowing to and saluting Madame Tussaud in wax!" But an uncontrollable thirst for alcoholic stimulants—a thirst for that vile poison, which has caused tears to flow sufficient to float a fleet of vessels, early removed him from life. May the giver of all good and perfect gifts, blot out his frailties, and the angel of mercy drop a tear of pity over his weakness.

CHAPTER XXV.

PRICES CURRENT—WHIG CONVENTION—SUNDAY AT THE MINES—THE WEATHER—QUARTZ MILLS—THE MISFORTUNE OF A SAN FRANCISCO MERCHANT.

Provisions were always sold by weight, and although much reduced in price, still they were not as low as many thought they ought to have been. Butter, made at Goshen, New York, retailed at 75 cents per pound; hams, Ohio sugar-cured, 25 to 35 cents; flour, 10 to 12 cents; potatoes, 12 cents; dried fruit, 30 cents; onions, 40 cents; pickles, from $1 to $1½ per bottle; fresh beef, when we could get it, 35 cents; mackerel, 38 cents each; sugar 25 to 30 cents; and molasses 50 cents a pint.

June 17th, 1851. The bell sounded, the citizens assembled together—for what? To nominate municipal officers.

Now, the larger number of citizens were decidedly opposed to our town being incorporated; a few designing and speculating men only desired it. Soon after the meeting was organized I took the floor, and moved that "it is inexpedient to nominate candidates for town officers," which was promptly seconded, unanimously adopted, and the *brilliant* convention adjourned *sine die*.

Wednesday, June 18th. To-day was held our first Whig convention; delegates from Nevada and Rough and Ready joined us. My friend, Judge S——, of whom I have heretofore spoken, was unanimously elected presiding officer; and the entire proceedings reminded me very much of the political conventions I had attended as "lobby member" in the eastern states. There was considerable discussion in relation to the office of State senator. Nevada wanted the candidate selected from her district. Rough and Ready very modestly withdrew from the discussion, and finally it was compromised by our district getting the senatorial nominee, and Nevada taking the lion's share of the candidates for the assembly.

During the morning *Captain* Wemah, head chief of the Indian tribe in our valley, came into the room, and as he took a seat alongside of me, I watched his countenance, feeling curious to know how the proceedings would interest him. The old chief understood about as much of the English language as a Japanese. He sat silent awhile, gazed all around the room, rose up, straightened himself, turned around, exclaimed "ugh," and off he marched.

Mr. John A. C——, whose lectures upon gambling and intemperance were noticed in previous chapters, was nominated for senator. Three candidates for the assembly were nominated—two taken from Nevada, and one from Rough and Ready. As usual on such occasions, the nominations were declared the unanimous choice of the convention; each candidate pledged himself as thoroughly devoted to Whig measures, the entire convention promised to work faithfully and unceasingly for the success of the Whig ticket, and with three cheers and *a tiger*, the assembly separated in the best humor.

Sunday, June 22d. The weather, as usual, lovely.— Everybody appeared good-humored, and gladly rested from the fatiguing duties of the past week. There was no preaching or lecturing, no ringing of church bells, no Sabbath Schools, each one was free to do and act as he pleased. Over there, under the sheltering branches of a tall oak, are seated a crowd of miners, with their sun-burnt faces, almost concealed from view by their heavy moustaches and whiskers, listening to that delicate looking man relating his early trials in gold hunting; now they laugh, anon they look serious. And there go a party on a prospecting tour; here pass by a crowd of "jolly good fellows" bound for Nevada to spend the day. Look! the stores are open—what a trade is carried on ; see that man purchasing clothing, and that one laying in a stock of provisions, perhaps each one would have scorned the idea of trading on the Sabbath, had they been at home, but custom makes strange beings of us all.

Look through the cabin doors of some of the miners and see how busily employed they are : there sits one mending his clothing, another washing, and another reading a well worn letter, perhaps from his mother—or from one, to marry whom he risked everything to reach California, and there accumulate sufficient to enable him to wed.

Now it is noon-day—the men separate one by one, partake of a lunch, then read, and finally stretch themselves on the ground and sleep sweetly, dreaming, perhaps, of the happy home they left, or blest with bright visions of success, and a happy re-union of dear friends. But the sun has gone down behind the long range of hills, supper is prepared, twilight always lovely and soothing, but especially so on a Sabbath eve, sets in. The chirping from a thousand evening insects is heard, night hovers over the village, another Sunday has gone by, and all is quiet.

Monday, June 23d.—The weather is now uncomfortably warm ; the water is fast drying up in the ravines, and most of the miners turning their attention to quartz digging. Let us go down Mill street and examine the quartz mills. See that pile of stones ! each one contains gold.

Watch that man how he breaks into small pieces the large stones; see, another shovels it into those large iron mortars; there are twelve mortars in the mill. Now the mill is in operation; see those heavy iron pestles how they descend into the mortars, crushing the stones to a coarse powder. A small stream of water is made to run through each mortar, which carries off the powdered rock into a large trough lined with muslin, the bottom covered with quicksilver. The gold being the heaviest, sinks to the bottom, the gravel passes over; and thump, thump, thump, is heard all day. At evening the mill is stopped, the gold is carefully scooped out, taken to the retort room, where it is separated from the mercury, and—that is all we can see.

Continuing my sketch of California acquaintances, I introduce a son of the Emerald Isle. He was a baker by trade, emigrated to California in 1848, found employment as journeyman baker at exorbitant wages, saved his money, and managed his finances so successfully, that he returned to New York worth over $15,000; traveled over a large portion of the states, but his previous habits and education prevented him from locating and investing his money judiciously. He must again venture to California, and seek the novelty, freedom and excitement that he enjoyed in San Francisco. Wages he found greatly reduced, and a man of his means could not hire out as a journeyman. So he rented the lower store-room of the Tontine buildings, invested his money in groceries, did a flourishing business, and was happy.

One night, when he had closed his store, and joined some acquaintances in strolling around the city to "see the sights," a cry of fire was raised. Fire! fire!! fire!!! the very sound was terrifying in San Francisco, for her citizens had suffered so severely. The whole male population turned out; fire, fire! run, men, "see that light," it's down on the wharf.

Patrick was frightened; on, on, he ran, he turned the corner—"what! the Tontine on fire?" "Here, men, lend a hand, save my goods; stand back." See, the building tumbles in, and in a few moments was a heap of hot cinders! I asked him if he saved any of his property? he answered, " I am not worth five dollars. '

CHAPTER XXVI.

GRAND INDIAN POW WOW OR CONVENTION—THE WEATHER —BRIEF ACCOUNT OF ANOTHER ACQUAINTANCE.

Look there! "Heigho, what is going on among the Indians?" Why, there is to be a grand "Pow Wow" at Wemah's camp to-night; "Let us go down." "Agreed."

I was anxious to be present at the beginning of the exercises, but waiting for some friends, whose business detained them later than they had expected, we arrived at the camp *just in time to be too late* for the grand war-dance, in which participated the entire assemblage of chiefs, braves and warriors, many of whom were representatives from distant tribes who had come to attend the all-important " big talk " in relation to the " pale faces."

The squaws were not allowed to indulge in any of the sports, neither were they permitted to come within speaking distance of the council house.

Some of the warriors were profusely decorated with fancy colored feathers, beads, shells and trinkets, and liberally daubed with paint. After resting a short time, the gaily-decked Indians made for the council chamber, (a description of which, and the camp, I gave in a former chapter,) which was dimly lighted by a fire in the centre, around which the various delegations squatted in a circle.

" Captain " Wemah, who held the important position of chief over all the Digger Indians, stood in the centre of the party, and when all were quiet—not a whisper to be heard—he commenced his opening and welcome speech, delivering it with wonderful fluency, great vehemence, and wild and violent gesticulations. During his *powerful* address, he was frequently applauded by his well behaved and respectful auditory. The old chief was dressed in his best suit: his coat, which had been given him by an American soldier, fitted him about as well as the garments that are put on a stick to frighten off the crows from a corn field; in one pocket he had a couple of empty bottles, in the other a huge horse pistol, which once might have been a formidable weapon, but now lacked a trigger! When he had concluded his speech, he called out—" Ven Wollupie "—" si, si, signor." Two stout, well-developed braves seized a tub of *daintily* prepared acorn gruel, and placed it before their delegation; others were called, who followed their example, until every squad was supplied with a tub of gruel; then, at the signal of the " Captain," each Indian dipped his unwashed hands into the delectable food, and gulped down the gruel like a half-starved pig.

After the liberal entertainment was finished, the *Convention or Pow Wow* was called to order, and Wemah again addressed the motley crowd, with even more earnestness than before. There were unmistakable evidences of discontent. The fire in the centre of the council house was fast dying out; the discussion waxed warm; those of the Indians who could not get inside of the chamber, clambered on the roof, and peeped down the hole in the middle, heedless of the smoke, and the vile stench which issued forth in murky clouds. Wemah danced, frothed and expostulated, but all to no purpose. The " Pow Wow " lost all sense of propriety, and the clever old chief stalked out in apparent disgust. No sooner had his " highness " retired, than every " pale face " inside the council was unceremoniously ordered out.

As a report of the great speech of the evening would doubtless be interesting, though not familiar with the Indian language, I will endeavor to give a few sentences from memory's log : " *Ingin—no cara—ugh—bah—manayna—he, ya, hi—mucho Americano fight—si hugh—capitaw—ugh fire-water, whiskey aqua no good—sleepy—ha—he—yes !* "

I passed around the camp, and stopped in front of Wemah's wigwam. There the old chief lay flat upon his face, his military coat buttoned up to his chin, around him the numerous ladies of his household. Just then a friend called to me; I looked around, and found I was the only " pale face " within the camp—the small hours of another day had come around. I hastened to join my companions, when we returned to our wigwams, and sought and found refreshing sleep.

The weather during this month (July) was oppressively warm ; it was almost impossible to work during the afternoon, but it made but little difference about working " on short time," for the water was getting scarce, and men could accomplish very little by ravine mining.

Continuing my account of California acquaintances, which exhibits the variety of characters, tastes and education of her population, I introduce the son of a Boston clergyman. This clever, fine-appearing young gentleman, at an early age, was afflicted with sore eyes; all the remedies suggested by friends and physicians were of no avail. He was an ambitious youth, and keenly felt the sore affliction. As a dernier resort, he was advised to take a European tour; he knew his father's limited pecuniary resources, and hesitated. Finally, that devoted father said: "Here, my son, are six hundred dollars; take this money and go to Europe, and perhaps your eyes may be restored to a healthy condition." He accepted, but to himself vowed that, if he lived, he would accept any occupation that was not disreputable, to refund that father his money; the sequel will show whether he did.

The day for bidding adieu to family and friends arrived; he bade " good bye," and sailed for England. Aware of his limited finances, he determined to practice economy. Through England, France, Germany and Italy he traveled, but nearly always on foot, with his knapsack fastened to his back. His fine carriage and gentlemanly deportment won " troops of friends, and he enjoyed his views afoot" exceedingly. Often he was supposed to be one of the Boston literati traveling in-cog; again he was taken for some wealthy gentleman traveling on foot, purposely to view the country more satisfactorily than he otherwise could by coach or railway.

He preserved his incognito; was often entertained by

nobles, and had abundant enjoyment. In Rome he hired a room—marble floor, comfortable bed, had his breakfast furnished him, also his boots blacked—all for one dollar a week. His dinner he procured at one of the numerous cafés for five cents.

Here he met gentlemen from Boston, and whenever invited to join them in their travels, he would respectfully decline, preferring to continue his travels alone and "afoot." His six hundred dollars were nearly exhausted, so he engaged passage in the first steamer up for America; returned to his friends improved in knowledge and general health, save his eyes, which still remained weak.

The California gold excitement broke out; accustomed to travel and excitement, he rushed to the land of " Oro."

The climate of California suited his constitution; he wrote home cheering accounts of the improved condition of his eyes, and his bright prospects of the future; and upon my inquiry whether he had transmitted any of his California earnings home, he exhibited to me receipts of drafts for over $2,000 which he had sent his father.]

CHAPTER XXVII.

THE WEATHER—A LAND-SLIDE—SHADE AND ORNAMENTAL TREES—CONSIDERABLE TALK ABOUT "THE POOR INDIAN."

August, 1851.—It is needless, almost, to make any observations concerning the weather during this month. I will only remark that no one who could avoid it, would leave the comfortable shade to toil under the burning rays of the sun. About 11 o'clock in the morning I would quit out-door work, and the ravines adjacent to Centerville presented a desolate scene—hardly a miner could be seen. As the water was insufficient to "run the machine," I employed a great portion of the time in hunting gold-bearing quartz, which was more a source of pleasure than toil. Sometimes I was very successful; I remember I had used a flat stone for several days about my trough, and one day in passing my claim, I picked up the same stone which I had frequently thrown aside; but this time I examined it closely, found it thoroughly injected with gold, reduced it to powder, and realized from it fourteen dollars. I also had a beautiful transparent piece of quartz, resembling one of the drops to a chandelier—in the centre was embedded a lump of gold—quite a curiosity, even in California.

Occasionally we would find pebbles cemented together, forming masses as hard as the solid rock, evidencing the fact of an internal fire at some period more remote than the oldest inhabitant's great, great-grandfather could recollect. The hill upon which my cabin was built was supposed to have been formed by a land-slide, for upon digging down to the depth of fifty feet, large pieces of charcoal were brought to light, injected with bright particles of sulphuret of iron, also pieces of stone which, upon close inspection, proved to be petrified wood. Very frequently pieces of gold would be found having a resemblance to animals and various fanciful figures, which specimens always sold at high prices, and were manufactured into breast pins, rings, and other ornaments.

Some of our citizens turned their attention to horticultural pursuits, and ultimately realized more money than by mining. Vegetables, in consequence of the richness of the soil, grew to almost monstrosities. Irrigation and ditching were resorted to by agriculturists during the dry season. At the time I am writing about, any person could have procured a farm for the trouble of fencing it in, and having it recorded at a cost of only three dollars.

When not mining, or otherwise profitably engaged, I amused myself in improving the outside of my lone cabin. I selected the prettiest young pine trees, cut them down, brought them to my cabin, and planted them in front of my door, until I had formed an arbor which afforded me a delightful shade, and made my retreat more private.

There grew on the hill a tree called the massinetto; the bark was smooth, of dark red color, the leaves light green, and the flowers white; it seemed a favorite tree for bees and little birds. I selected the prettiest and largest ones I could find, cut them down, dragged them to my house, dug holes, and planted them in front of the pine trees, and so long as the flowers were in bloom, I could boast of the prettiest arbor to be found around the settlement; and when I came forth from my cabin, I enjoyed not only my arbors, but more particularly the society of the many little birds and pretty winged insects that never failed to pay me morning visits.

During the month of August there were no religious services held in our district; still, those miners who had received religious instruction in their youth, always conducted themselves with proper decorum on the Sabbath—another evidence of the importance of parents training up their children correctly.

As respectable females were coming among us, and our settlement was becoming a place of considerable importance, a commendable improvement was observed in the habits and dress of the Red Men. Some of the squaws could be seen with frocks on, and the braves wearing hats and trowsers.

8

One day, observing several acquaintances laughing heartily, I inquired the cause of their mirth, when my attention was directed to a procession of three Indians coming up the street. The first warrior was playing the jewsharp, as unconcernedly as though he had been in his wigwam, having only an apron on; the next hero was whistling, turning neither to the right nor left, but walking ahead, regardless of the loud laughing of the " pale faces;" his entire dress consisted of an old vest, and that unbuttoned! The last Indian was singing; he strutted proudly by, clad in a hickory shirt which he valued above price.

Whenever an Indian visited a trading establishment, the most gaudy colored handkerchiefs, calicos, &c., were shown him. Indians never value money; and I have seen them enter a store, put down their gold dust, and keep on buying until the storekeeper would call out, "all gone."

I saw a finely developed brave come into one of the stores, gaze all around the room until his keen eye caught sight of a bundle of "Arctic" comforts, and although the weather was oppressively warm, he purchased several and wrapped them around his waist, and stalked out as proud as an emperor.

These Indians were generally men of truth; whenever an Indian requested a garment to be laid aside for him it was done, for the merchant felt sure that he would return on the promised day.

On one occasion, chief Wolupe, next in rank to Capt. Wemah, ordered a heavy cloth coat, and promised to call with the "oro" after two "sleepy;" after the two "sleepy" passed, in walked the chief, and with a distressed look, announced that "Injun man play push stick—lost him money, bah, ugh;" but he promised to come back again after one "sleepy," and he did and bought the coat. They are very fond of gambling, and use sticks instead of cards.

They are a temperate people, and afraid of "fire-water." They are a virtuous people, but, of course, like all human beings, their characters exhibit both good and bad traits. They never use salt on their meat; when game is brought into camp, it is thrown on the fire, roasted, and then greedily devoured, with little regard to the rules of conventional society.

Acorns are a favorite article of food, and a full supply is always kept on hand for emergencies. They are a dirty, filthy people. Their active out-door life, and abstinence from rich cooked dishes, preserve them from many ailments with which more civilized people are afflicted. The poor squaws are compelled to labor very hard. The warriors holding any kind of work in utter contempt, they had rather starve than be tied to labor. The squaws are never allowed to idle away their time; while some are employed in pounding acorns, the rest are sent out to search for esculent roots and vegetables. An acquaintance of mine expressed a desire to have a smart-looking Indian boy to live with him; he was accommodated, but after a couple of days' life among the "pale faces," Indian boy vamosed without saying, "by your leave, sir."

A couple of gentlemen wished to get up a grand Indian war-dance at Nevada, and while they would feast the Indians for their performance, they anticipated a considerable profit on the speculation. Captain Wemah acquiesced, and his whole tribe was soon preparing for the "first grand exhibition by native Indians;" and as Captain Wemah had always been friendly to the whites, he hoped for a full attendance.

Handbills were printed and distributed far and wide; great inducements set forth, and the price of tickets *only* two dollars each. One morning I was standing at the head of Mill street, and observed chief Wemah riding along on an old scraggy-looking pony, bowing to everybody, followed by his warriors, braves, squaws and little ones; nearly every squaw had a huge willow basket strapped to her back. Away they scampered in the happiest humor, bound for the exhibition. At night I saw the captain and his train returning in the worst humor. I asked him what was the matter? he replied: "Americana no good, bah!"

Some rowdy fellows had broken down the inclosure, stopped the performances; and the Indians were as mad

as California panthers. They, however, lost nothing—
they had plenty of fresh beef and bread; but the managers made a bad speculation—lost two hundred dollars. They had purchased several beeves, had them killed and dressed for the performers, but the rowdies interrupted the performances, and they sold no tickets.

CHAPTER XXVIII.
A GALLOP TO AUBURN AND BACK.

September, 1851. There were often litigations among miners, and I derived considerable revenue by acting as juror, for hardly a day passed that I was not summoned to appear before the honorable court, or be subjected to a fine of twenty-five dollars. On one occasion a party from Auburn (a mining settlement some thirty miles from Grass Valley) visited our place for the purpose of procuring a witness whose knowledge of the *modus operandi* of quartz claims could be relied upon. It so happened that the party chanced to stop at my friend C———'s store, and upon making known the object of their visit to Grass Valley, were referred to the recorder of Cardinal Hill. I learned from them that the difficulty was about the priority of possession of a supposed valuable claim,—that one party claimed to be the discoverers of gold-bearing quartz near Auburn, and that during their necessary absence at San Francisco to procure money and tools, another party took forcible possession and refused to yield up the claim. I remarked that my knowledge of the working of quartz claims was reliable, for I assisted in framing the laws of our hill, that the rules of working, and the protection each miner enjoyed were embraced in said laws. Further than that " deponent saith not." However, I was solicited " to come over," state before the " learned court" what I knew, and that my entire expenses would be paid, and I also receive the usual fees " made and provided," etc.

Having no very urgent business to detain me, and in humor for a jaunt, I hired John the baker's favorite nag Bob, and started at a fine pace. I had never traveled over that road before, and when I was about five miles from home, I hardly knew whether I was going right or wrong. I saw in the almost hidden path no person or living thing, but snakes, tule and luxuriant growing grass, and between Bob and myself, I thought I had lost my way; however, I whipped up Bobby, and kept on a straight course " due south," until I overtook a man standing like a statue beneath the friendly sheltering branches of a large tree. I inquired the route to Auburn, etc.; he replied, " all right—keep right straight on."

Away I galloped, but I stopped again; now there were two paths, and which was the " straight on " one I was puzzled to know, so I halted awhile; soon a traveler came along, and I asked his assistance. He said: " take that path; bad road, sir; hurry up—better not let night overtake you,"

I took *that* path, but it occurred to me that his advice coincided with the information a friend had imparted, relative to a suspicious house midway. Now, I am not a nervous man, nor am I a fighting man, but I observed the strictest watch, for I well knew that lawless and vicious men were prowling around, and in addition to this, I did not know the person who desired my testimony, and further, I was known to travel alone and unarmed; but my cause was a just one, and I determined to see the end of my journey. On—on I spurred my faithful nag until I came near the suspected locality, where I had been told *travelers had taken suddenly sick and died.* Now, it may appear a trifling matter to those persons surrounded by friends, and enjoying the privileges of a civilized community, but I am free to declare that the bravest of the brave, under like circumstances, would have paused to consider and prepare.

I never carried a pistol in my life; I never assaulted any one; but I always trusted in the protection of our heavenly Father. As soon as I emerged from the rank, luxuriant tule, and faced the spotted house, men came towards me, and offered inducements for me to alight, but my business was urgent, my horse was restless, and away I galloped; now crossing ditches, now ascending hills, then dashing through thick forests, until I was about to ascend a long, gently rising hill, so common in California, and here I allowed Bob to take his time, whilst I gazed with delight upon the charming scenery spread out before me.

At the summit of the mountain I found the "traveler's rest"—a shingle hut—and as the weather was oppressively warm, and Bobby had performed his part well, and needed rest, I dismounted, tied him under the branches of a venerable elm tree, fed him on barley, fresh from the field, gave him pure mountain water, partook of refreshment myself, and rested for some time. The day was fast waning, and yet I was a considerable distance from Auburn. The landlord told me I could reach it before dark. I mounted Bobby, bade adieu to the landlord of the "mountain cottage," and followed the well-beaten path until it was lost to view; this was inexplicable to me, but riding "straight on" I overtook a solitary miner, who informed me that "when I rounded yonder hill, Auburn would not be a mile off."

Thanking him, I spurred up Bob, and thought of that lone miner—perhaps he was working for the support of aged parents; perhaps for the successful accomplishment of some cherished object; but hark! I hear yells and a loud noise. Bobby snorted and galloped faster; we "rounded yonder hill," and looking down the valley, I saw Auburn below us.

Bobby trotted on, and I espied on a log cabin in huge capital letters, "The Empire Hotel." Before I reached the "Empire," I heard some one cry out, "Doctor, doctor—this way, sir." I followed "this way," and found my employer for the nonce waiting for me, who conducted me to the hotel, and gave instructions to the "empress of the log cabin" to furnish the doctor with the very best, and always refuse any money tendered by him. This cordial reception was gratifying. I had "sir Robert" properly cared for, and by the time I had washed my face and hands the supper bell sounded, and I sat down to an excellent meal, evidencing a capable landlady.

Afterwards I strolled around the city, and pronounced it the dirtiest, most ill-looking, wo-begone village or settlement it had ever fell to my lot to visit. I returned to the hotel, and soon engaged in friendly conversation with my clever hostess, who was fresh from Ireland's green sod, and who very politely invited the doctor to take "a wee drop of the cratur' to strengthen him;" *siveral gintlemen* from ould Ireland hoped "the stranger would not refuse to take a little drop of *whuskey* with them." Many of the boarders were curious to know who that *spectacled stranger* was; some thought him a "judge,"

8*

others a "pracher," and not a few "one of the vagilance committee men;" however, the night was advancing—I felt fatigued, and signified a desire to go to sleep. I could not, with propriety, say, go tobed, for very few enjoyed that luxury. My hostess conducted me to a nice, clean cot, into which I soon jumped, and slept that night for the first time in many months between sheets; but I did not fall into sound sleep until the wee hours of morning had come around; the boarders were so hilarious that I was continually aroused by three cheers for our side, etc. However, I finally fell into a profound sleep, and when I awoke, daylight had entered my apartment, which contained sleeping accommodations for *only* forty travelers.

The party who had engaged me to "come over and attend court," told me during the morning that the "case would not come off," as there was a probability of compromising the difficulty, and my services were not needed. I rejoiced at this *wise* conclusion of the disputants, for I was anxious to get home in time for our county election to come off next day. I had my faithful nag brought out, and about 10 o'clock bade all a cordial good-bye, and started off in the finest style—having made by the visit, for doing nothing, over $13 clear of all expenses.

I knew the road this time, and Bob seemed glad to get back. Woa, woa, what's the matter now? Oh! I see, a detachment of Indians are coming, and Bob is frightened;

but I patted him on the neck—cordially saluted the Indians—Bob galloped on, and I let him "go ahead" until we reached the halfway house, which was only a temporary tent that could be taken down and put up in forty minutes. Here I gave Robert his dinner, and then resumed my journey. Just at the rise of the first mountain I heard some one call out to me "to stop," and upon looking around I saw a ferocious-looking human biped, who again ordered me to stop. I knew his object, and giving whip and spurs to Bobby, I left the gentleman far behind.

The road was now getting more distinct; I knew where I was, not far from home on the "hill top." I permitted Robert to feed by the wayside; but the sun had gone down; I spurred on, and soon reached Grass Valley, where a host of friends gladly welcomed me back, for they felt anxious concerning my safety, and still more anxious about losing my vote next day.

CHAPTER XXIX.

AN ELECTION—CENTREVILLE RAVINE—ENERGY OF GOLD SEEKERS—THEIR HOPES—LAW MATTERS, Etc.

September, 1851. In a former chapter I gave an account of the first Whig convention held in Grass Valley, of the unanimity which prevailed, and of the pledge each member gave of working faithfully and thoroughly for the party. Well, on Wednesday 4th, the election came off, and the Whig and Democratic parties buckled on their armor, and battled with a will for their favorite candidates. The weather was propitious, and every man that could be scared up, was brought to the polls and made to exercise the prerogative of which freemen delight to boast. I remember a laughable incident that occurred just before the polls closed. The Whig candidates had misgivings as to the result. It is said, "straws show which way the wind blows," and so not a few of us thought the gallant Whig party would come off second best.

Mr. C———, the Whig senatorial nominee, called upon his friends and urged them " to keep on until the polls closed, for the opposition were very active." Happening to look down Mill street, I observed two men approaching, who were at once accosted by Captain R——— with the inquiry, " whether they had voted yet?" They replied, "no sir, we are not entitled to a vote; but if we did vote, it would be for the whole Democratic ticket." The Captain quickly tore off the word Whig from a ticket, and said, "Come, gentlemen, you are privileged to exercise the elective franchise, for the other party allow anybody to vote." So off they marched, Captain R.·———, the Whig partisan, in high glee, and as they neared the polls, some one cried out, " Clear the way—let these gentlemen vote." Just then a Democratic sentinel sang out, " I challenge them men, sir." Captain R———, like the Democratic watchman, was pretty well soaked with " bittersweet," and instantly turned round, manifesting the most violent rage, asked, " What right have you to interfere with these gentlemen?" " None of your business, sir. Here, strangers, what ticket do you vote?" " Why, sir, if we can vote, we go the entire Democracy." Here, then, was laughter, and a terrible fuss created around the polls. Six o'clock, the time for closing, was drawing nigh. Democrats explained to the strangers the trick about to be played upon them, and amid swearing, quarrelling, and wrangling, they voted—the Democratic ticket! and the applause and vehement cheering of our opponents was enough to enrage the whole Whig party, who, however, took it in good part, and acknowledged they were outgeneraled.

During the evening the result of the election was announced, and our gallant Whig party was routed—terribly routed.

A meeting of miners holding claims on the Centreville ravine, was held on the evening of the 8th. The preamble and resolutions I offered were adopted. I knew they would be, for at every meeting, no matter where held, the resolutions which are prepared in advance, then read to the meeting, are generally unanimously adopted.

Our claims were extended to sixty feet square. This was the most important resolution, and a committee was appointed to survey the ravine and select a site for a ditch. I was chairman of the committee, and *a most excellent selection it was,* for I knew as much about canals and ditches as I did of the verbs and adverbs of the Hottentot lingo. However, the committee next day commenced operations, surveyed the ravine and followed the water course for several miles, and after consultation, arrived at the *sage* conclusion " that our claims would only hold out for another season, and the rainy season would soon be upon us; we respectfully recommend that we leave well enough alone, and the *learned* committee be discharged."

But seriously speaking, California has exhibited the leading traits and indomitable energies of the American people. The miners accomplished wonders. Think of men unaccustomed to hard work, turning rapid running rivers from the natural channel; think of mountains excavated with only pick and shovel; think of villages built up with the rapidity of magic almost; think of land, which had never before been upturned, now teeming with barley, oats, wheat, rye, and corn; think of steamers plying the beautiful streams, of elegant suburban retreats, of farms laid off, and thrift, and abundance everywhere manifest; think of Sierra Nevada itself penetrated to the very centre by the American people, and all this accomplished in a few years, no wonder their indomitable energy and unflagging perseverance have surprised and astonished the world.

Professors of Colleges, ministers of the Gospel, lawyers, doctors, judges, mechanics, merchants, and bankers, working with a determination and energy worthy of success. No false distinctions of society; no mushroom aristocratic notions tolerated; muscle, bone, and sinew were everything; but yet the cultivated mind availed much, for those possessing well trained intellects were enabled to endure cheerfully the greatest exposures and the severest hardships.

Towards the close of the month the weather assumed a more agreeable temperature; the sky, which appeared so clear and azure-hued for many, many months, now began to change, denoting, what a miner most ardently desires, the approach of the season of rain and storms. Now the absent miners return; now our village presents a more cheerful appearance; claims that were deserted are being "jumped" by new comers, and claims which yielded well and were watched over by the miners during the summer months, are being restaked, and active preparations going on for the ensuing winter. Tradesmen have returned with replenished stock, and all are congratulating themselves upon the hope of securing, the coming season, sufficient of the glittering dust to enable them to say, " in a few days I am off for home."

If ever men deserved success, the California gold seekers did; those especially who were among the pioneers of the "emigrants"—those who, amid various hardships and unwritten miseries, kept up, hoped on, hoped ever— and those also who " prospected " along the beautiful and picturesque valleys where civilized man had never before trod—where the commonest necessaries of life could hardly be obtained, but pushing ahead, enduring every deprivation, hoping, still hoping to secure the prize.

It is very common for speakers to say, " Oh, how men will rush to the land of gold and endure every hardship to secure filthy lucre, and yet give so little attention to the salvation of their souls." But men must put forth all their energies to gain a subsistence—must earn money to support themselves and families, and if they can secure a competence sooner by rushing to California, the sooner they can afford a comfortable support to aged parents, a wife, a child, or even to some benevolent institution; and men do not always forget their religious education by striving to earn money; the truth is, every one of us, ministers and tradesmen, would not refuse opportunities for accumulating money for the benefit of ourselves and families—and there is nothing sinful in so doing : the only sin is in the misapplication of money and the inordinate love of it.

Rev. Mr. Williams, of the Presbyterian church, preached for us on Sunday 14th, morning and evening. The attendance was good, the preacher's remarks acceptable, and the order and decorum commendable.

During this month I served as a juror in many "cases at law," which were chiefly brought about by disputes regarding claims, etc.

On one occasion, in the necessary absence of Judge S―――― from our district, the most learned judge in the valley, a suit for damage was brought before Judge M――, who held court in his kitchen, as the other " spare room the women folks wanted." The jury consisted of three members, each of whom were " full of fun, fancy, and drollery." When the jury agreed upon their verdict, the learned esquire said : " Gentlemen of the jury, please hand me your verdict." The foreman instantly arose and replied : " May it please your honor, I am instructed by my fellow-jurors to demand their fees prior to rendering the verdict." What's this? his honor was startled; demanding the verdict, and told he must produce the fee first; the learned judge demurred; he had not so understood the law. "Perhaps, may it please the honorable court, your honor has not *reached* that part of the law, made and provided in such cases," replied a juror. His honor (who was really a kind-hearted, well-meaning man, but sadly deficient in matters of law,) readjusted his heavy-framed German silver spectacles, wet the tips of his fingers, turned over the leaves of a huge law book, and— held the matter under advisement, becoming personally responsible to the jurors for their fees!

Some time afterward his honor informed us " that he had consulted with gentlemen learned in law, and they had pronounced the jury sustained by the book; but still, he thought it a mighty queer rule."

CHAPTER XXX.

A CHANGE IN THE WEATHER—CALIFORNIAN'S HOPES AND TRIALS—A LAW CASE—SIGN PAINTING, Etc., Etc.

October, 1851. Three cheers! The temperature is cool and delicious, the cerulean sky has disappeared, and now murky clouds are hovering over our village. Congratulations are exchanged by the anxious miners, bright visions of distant homes are rising up, and shovel, pick, and spade, are the order of the day. "Come, boys, clean up your claims—prepare for a last trial; the rain will be upon us soon, and let us all be prepared." I, too, surveyed my claim, and began to "throw off top dirt." Talk of the pleasures of hope. Why, sir, learn from Californians what hope is! Pleasures of memory! ask a Californian. Oh, how I have rejoiced when some adventurous spirit has accumulated his "pile," and was enabled to exclaim, "Good bye, friends; I am bound for home, with my wash bowl—in my eye." It may seem strange to your readers, who have always lived at home, surrounded with the comforts and luxuries of life, that so much talk should be made by Californians about home, comfort, and happiness, but ah! could each Californian relate his trials, his sufferings, his exposures, and his hopes and fears, what harrowing tales would be unfolded. Some have been disappointed, some have succeeded, and others have found a resting place by the hill-side; others sleep their last sleep on the far-spreading plains and prairies, where no friend visits the grave, or plants the rose or lowly violet on their hurriedly made sepulchres. Some, that fail, lack the courage to return to their friends, but work on, work on, living only in hope and the pleasurable anticipation of soon finding the "big lump." There is once source of happiness to the Californian, which can never be fully understood by friends at home; I allude to letters—to a sheet of paper, scribbled over, perhaps, carelessly by a friend, who little thinks how each word, each crossing of the T, or dotting of an I, will be dwelt upon; how every sentence is remembered, and how the rough miner throws his body down on his hard pallet, with his letter secreted in his bosom, and dreams, perchance, of the writer, or of the pleasure of returning home, and embracing friends from whom he has so long been absent.

So far as mining operations were concerned, I attended to very little during this month; in fact, I had other business to engage my attention which was more profitable and genial to my feelings; still, I held on to my claims, and worked just when I felt disposed. But the facilities for procuring a constant supply of water throughout the mining districts are now so complete that miners have vastly the advantage over those who worked at the time

I am writing about; so also with regard to mining implements. Now improved machinery and increased knowledge of working claims, together with the ease of procuring the necessaries of life, render a miner's life much more comfortable, than it was during my sojourn in the "land of gold."

As I was ready and willing to do anything not disreputable to add to my "bank account," I had applications to perform sundry work, most of which was "Greek to me." On one occasion, an acquaintance of mine hired a horse for a day of an exceedingly cross-grained, ill-natured, thick-pated fellow, who charged my friend with cruelly treating his horse, and sued him at court, laying damages at one hundred dollars. Now, what was to be done? Why, "employ a friend learned in law to manage the case." And *who was the learned attorney selected but myself.* Though frequent and unexpected demands were made upon me, this request of helping a friend out of difficulty in a suit at law, *took me all aback.* However, I recovered myself, and determined to carry out my resolve of attending to any business with which I might be entrusted. The papers were handed me. I looked them over, and really, everything seemed more difficult than reading Hebrew poetry. I told the judge that he might anticipate a rare treat, for I was going to "astonish the crowd with my maiden speech." His honor was delighted, and promised all the assistance I might require. Before the hour for "spouting" arrived, I gave notice to my friends to be on hand at the justice's office, and I would furnish them with fine sport, for I had undertaken the profession of law, and was about to defend my client at all hazards.

Now for the joke of the story. When I appeared in the court-room, armed with papers, documents, and surcharged with a *fiery* speech, what should I see but my client sitting side by side with a magistrate in close conversation, evidently about to settle the case without the *learned counsel's advice.* A significant nod from my friend told me a compromise was going on, and instead of practicing law, I *was sworn in as constable,* and ordered to summon six good and reliable citizens to appear before the honorable court in twenty-five minutes or be subjected, the whole posse of us, to a fine of twenty-five dollars each. "Oh, what a fall was there, my countrymen!"

I obeyed the order of the court, and brought in six "good and reliable citizens," most of whom tried to beg off, but the court, through its "indefatigable police," must be obeyed. The result of the matter was a satisfactory compromise without going to trial, an exorbitant fee paid over to the constable (myself) from my client, and a recommendation from the honorable court to "let off my speech on the next Fourth of July."

Sometimes I tried my hand at sign-painting, receiving

only fifty cents a letter—and such letters! The first sign I was ordered to paint was for a grocery establishment; there were three partners, and not having much experience in the painting business, I could not tell how much muslin was required, as I had not decided upon the size of the letters. So I managed in this way—a friend allowed me to take a piece of musin and chalk off the letters, and then cut off the quantity needed. When I had marked off half the letters, I had to stop again to measure the house, lest I might have the sign wider than the house; but I hit the width pretty well, and in due time had the sign ready for the paint. Well, where could I procure the paint and brushes? Ah, another friend came to my rescue, and soon I was daubing the muslin *secundum artem*, finished the sign, tacked it up, amid the cheers and quizzing remarks of my friends who were standing below enjoying the scene.

The same firm had another order for me, to paint them in large letters, " Hay, oats and barley for sale here." I commenced it at once, and the next day I was paid partly in money and partly in groceries, and my larder was better filled than at any time previously during my stay in California.

CHAPTER XXXI.

THE WEATHER—BURGLARS—A BLACK BEAR AROUND—A PARTY OF PLEASURE.

November, 1851. The dry season seemed interminable. Only occasional showers during this month, and many were under the impression that if the rain did not pour down very soon, we might, indeed, " hang up our pick and shovel." The temperature was agreeable; the sun, which had shone forth so brilliantly, unobstructed by a single passing cloud, was now frequently obscured from view by dark clouds, which threatened heavy rains. But the men exercised commendable patience, and very many who were loudest in their complaints at the absence of water, were uncertain of more than paying expenses, if the ravines had been full of water. But all had their hopes, and each man would have been rejoiced to witness the success of his friend ; for the peculiar life of a Californian made us all a community of friends.

There are many laughable incidents connected with my life in California, and what may now appear ludicrous and mirth-provoking, then seemed hard and almost insupportable. We were all very much annoyed by rats which infested our cabins, and various were the expedients resorted to, to rid us of our troublesome guests. Some of my acquaintances constructed "dead falls," and had the satisfaction of finding every morning several rats completely trapped.

One night I thought I heard some one in my cabin. I was all alone on the hill—had neither gun nor pistol, nor even a thimble-full of powder. I sang out, "Who is there?" No answer. Just then down tumbled a fine ham I had just purchased. Ah, you thieves! I'll catch you now. I struck a light, looked all around, but no one was in sight; I examined the ham, and soon cleared up the mystery in this way—viz.: I had tied a string to the ham, and suspended it about a foot from the rafter, so that Mr. Rat could not reach it; but the cunning thief took the matter into consideration, crept along the rafter, and doubtless thought, "I'll just gnaw the string, down will tumble the ham, and then I can follow after and eat my fill." But Mr. Rat was unacquainted with the science of acoustics, for the fall of the meat aroused me, and "I saved my bacon."

On another night a furious storm was raging, and everybody comfortably housed, or ought to have been, and although the rain was beating hard upon the roof of my cabin, and blowing through the crevices, I still anticipated a refreshing night's rest, and doubtless would have slept soundly until "broad daylight," had not "an alarming midnight" scene occurred, which aroused me so thor-

9

oughly from my slumbers that I did not care to sleep again that night.

I was lying upon my back enjoying a delightful nap, when suddenly down tumbled one, two, three, rascally, cowardly burglars on top of me. I sprang up, and a terrible fuss was made in my cabin. The intruders knew they aroused me, and were trying their best to escape, and the balance of their companions were rushing madly over the roof. By the time I struck a light the scamps were off, and on reconnoitering, I found that my disturbers were big Norway rats, who were " traveling around," or else seeking shelter from the storm, and chanced to get on my roof, and *without intending it*, broke through the shingles, and were, perhaps, more frightened than I was myself. But the rain was pouring in much too fast, so I had to go out, hunt up boards, or anything else convenient, that would answer to stop the leak, and all the satisfaction I could get in relating my misfortunes to my neighbors was a hearty " haw, haw, haw ! "

But on another evening I found an opportunity to turn the laugh upon my neighbors. I was sleeping at a " 2.40 " rate when rap, rap, rap, was sounded at my door. I called out, who's there ? " Get up, get up—a huge bear is around my cabin, and we'll have a fine chance to kill him." Well, kill him then ; he does not trouble me, and beside, I have neither gun nor pistol. " Well, get up at any rate."

I arose from my downy—I should say, pine-stem couch—looked out, but it was as dark as Iser; however, we sallied out—" brave Saxon warriors"—looked here and there, but no Mr. Bruin could we see, and I teased the party for a long time, declaring they took a "lame duck" for a black bear!

As our population increased, some amusement was necessary to render our stay in the mountains agreeable. The long evenings were tedious. Young men longed for sport and pleasant recreations; and I will here remark, then and there would have been the opportunity to have started prayer-meetings; then would have been the time to have exercised the mind upon holy and righteous matters; but we had no pious missionaries among us; men acted according to their earlier training, and I cheerfully accord to them the highest credit for conducting themselves honorably and gentlemanly, and with pleasure give my testimony to the correct deportment and honorable bearing at all times evinced by American travelers.

Well, any little excitement was always agreeable to the permanent population, and when it was announced that the "Alta Saloon" would open with a fashionable cotillion party, our youth of both sexes were delighted. I had never attended, up to that time, a "Ball" in my life, and could have been put down as a " green one."

On Tuesday 18th, the Ball took place, and as many

persons are not acquainted with the modus operandi of balls, cotillion parties, etc,, I will daguerreotype, for their benefit, ours. After nine o'clock, the ladies and their gallants began to assemble; in the meanwhile, the rougher sex were indulging in the "ardent." About 10 o'clock the leader of the orchestra gave the signal, the band struck up Washington's March, and the company formed in line, and marched into the hall two by two. After they had paraded around for some time, they were dismissed, only to be instantly summoned together by the floor manager, who sang out—"Make ready for a Spanish dance," whew! how the youth and *beauty* rushed to the floor, and stood like statuary awaiting the signal to trip it on "the light fantastic toe."

Such bowing and smiling as each participant extended to the other seemed excessively Frenchy and ludicrous. The violin sounded, and away flew the dancers, now here, now there, and then "way over yonder," which almost bewildered the verdant "looker-on." I expected every moment *they would run over each other*, but they didn't; and when the cotillion was over, they appeared as fresh and delighted as though they had not been exercising at all. And the dancing was kept up until midnight, when the whole party marched in procession across the street to the "Beatty House," and partook of an elegant supper, "which was fit for a king to enjoy." After eating and drinking, the company returned to the ball-room, and continued their dancing and pleasure until daylight; every one seemed to have enjoyed the evening entertainment, and I know I enjoyed a comfortable nap the next morning.

CHAPTER XXXII.

THE WEATHER — APPEARANCE OF CENTREVILLE RAVINE DURING THE MINING SEASON—A WALK IN THE DARK, AND A LEAP INTO THE CREEK.

December, 1851. In my last chapter I mentioned that every one was anxiously hoping for heavy rains to fill the creeks and ravines, and sure enough, if it came later than wished for, the gates of heaven seemed to have opened this month, and everything was as thoroughly saturated as though it had been raining for the last ten months. During this month I found my elegant cabin about as comfortable as a house without a roof. The wind blew hard, and consequently drove the rain through the numerous crevices, extinguishing my fire, preventing me from making coffee, and to add to my misfortunes, my Chinese-looking chimney could not withstand the wind and rain, and down it tumbled " sans ceremonie," compelling me to undergo a shower-bath while repairing it.

During the earlier part of the month I frequently found

the water in my bucket covered with ice; and those mornings when the storm appeared most violent I, like many others, remained in bed, deeming it the most comfortable quarters.

Well, the creeks and ravines soon afforded water to start the machines, and if ever men worked industriously, those men were the Centreville ravine miners; for they well knew, from the location of the ravine, a supply of water could only be depended upon for one or two months. What a sight for the uninitiated to look upon! what an interesting panorama was presented to the stranger in that same Centreville ravine during the "wet season." Over there a party of men "kiotying," digging down some ten or fifteen feet following the "lead," carefully throwing back the dirt, then hauling it to the top, and then running it through the "long-tom" in "less than no time." Still further over there a party of Kentuckians working away in the happiest humor—standing in mud, pitching up the dirt and stones, and washing it out; and hear that loud laugh—see those men dancing around, and as happy as mortals can be; why, they are the slaves of that tall Kentuckian—they love their master, they know no care nor trouble, and seem to live upon the rule—that " sufficient unto the day is the evil thereof;" and next to these are two young men from Ohio; they heed not the heavy rain; they work from early dawn until twilight; they have promised their families to return home next summer, and if hard work, and judicious deportment avail, they are safe for a delightful reunion with friends who may doubtless be counting the days and hours yet to intervene before they expect to reach their "home, sweet home." See that party of happy and cheerful young men to the right of the ravine—don't they work with a will? Not a man of the party had ever handled the pick or shovel before, but they work steadily, and diffuse a cheerful feeling all around them. They are from "down east." And hear that other party near by them; Ah, don't they take it easy? How they talk, laugh, and wrangle; why they are blacks, and were it not for the influence of their white neighbors, I question whether they would work at all.

Mount that pile of stones and look around you. Here comes the water dashing along, not, however, without being tapped by a hundred men, every one of whom is toiling, sweating and exposing himself in the rain, but never mind, the climate is healthy, and the cry is heard, "Boys, now is your chance or never." But see, the men quit work—the ravine is deserted; look up, see the smoke issuing from the fancifully built chimneys of the various rudely-constructed cabins—the miners are preparing dinner. After awhile they return to their work; the rain is still pouring down, but it does not prevent the miners from working; splash, toss, pitch, and shovel, are re-echoed through the woods the entire afternoon; and now as the day wanes, and the work is over, each one looks anxiously at the " ripple box," the tell-tale of their day's labor. The majority go to their cabins; a few remain at their claims to "pan out."

By-and-by the ravine is deserted; the shades of night are lowering over the village of huts; all around is dark and still; there, a light is struck in the cabin yonder— what a blazing fire! the miners are drying their clothes, preparing their supper, and dividing their day's profit. Let us look in upon them; the supper is over, the dishes are hastily placed in an old box, the pipes are lit, the wearied miners are enjoying their rest—one reads, another mends his clothes, another examines his pistols, and the rest talk, sing, and "kill time" as best suits them. Let us go further; never mind the storm. Look out! you are nearing a deep hole; stand back; get down on all fours; feel your way; why, where are you? never mind; now, get up, we have passed the most dangerous holes; the town is near, let us stroll around and observe the movements of the people. What building is that? why, that is the Beatty House; the stage stops there; it is *the hotel* of the town; our fast young men "do most congregate there." But where is that music? look across the street, don't you see that elegant saloon? Did you suppose that we, high up in the mountains, supported such a fine establishment? Come, we will enter; see how beautiful, what tasteful paper covers the walls; how elegant the whole room appears; what comfortable seats; what strong temptations to the unwary; see, those tables are loaded with pure, genuine coin; those men, looking so clever and cheerful, are professional gamblers, and the rest standing around are betting and losing their hard-earned money. But come, let us leave the excited crowd and seek our cabins.

My friend Young occasionally occupied an old cabin adjoining mine, and when my duties detained me "down town" until a late hour, friend Young would wait for me and act as an escort. I had told him of the great difficulty of reaching my cabin, for the nights were dark and the road so cut up by the miners, that twice the time was consumed in returning home at night." "Oh, my dear sir," Young would say, "I can pilot you along the holes and ditches almost as well as by daylight." So one night after a furious rain storm, which filled the holes and ditches with water, Young and I started for our cabins. The night was dark, so dark that we could not see our hand before us. "Come along, doctor, I'll guide you safe, just follow me." On we walked at the *fast rate of Brazilian sloths* until we came to a ditch about two feet wide, filled about three feet deep with water. I knew the place, for I had crossed it before; my plan was to give a

9*

vigorous jump, and then get down on all fours, and cross a temporary bridge some miners had erected for their special convenience; but that night I humored my friend, and allowed him to have his own way. "Stand still, doctor, here is a *creek*, you will have to jump; keep firm and and you will land safe." I soon discovered my pilot was nonplussed, but I let him take his own way. He stopped, then straightened himself, and jumped right plump into the water. I fell back laughing; I could not help it; but soon recovered myself, and assisted him out. Whilst he was lamenting his bad piloting, I prepared for a jump. Now, Colonel, stand back there! I cleared the stream, and stood safe on the opposite bank; but both of us were compelled to crawl and feel our way. Hold up, Young; keep still, I am on the edge of a deep hole. Now, keep to the right, a few more paces and we are safe. Ever afterward my friend carried a lantern, and we reached our cabins with more ease. The reason that I carried no light was because I was usually the sole occupant of the mountain, and I was supposed to carry money about me; and to tell the truth, I feared bad men more than I did a tumble into a ditch!

CHAPTER XXXIII.

THE NEW YEAR—RETURN OF FORMER CITIZENS—NEWS-
PAPERS—MISHAPS AND FATAL RESULTS.

January, 1852. Here commenced another year, and like many others, I asked myself, where shall I be at its close! and were I to scribble down but a moiety of the reflections which occurred to me then, I should fill this chapter with a dull sermon, interesting only to the writer. But abruptly dismissing the subject, I proceed at once to write out the various incidents that came under a miner's observation and experience.

First in order come the remarks on the weather, probably uninteresting to the general reader—but as a "faithful journalist" I must "make my observations." We had supposed that this month would have brought a succession of rain and storms—we had expected that, until the close of the mining season, every ditch and creek would have overflown with water; but not so. We had very little rain, and as lovely weather as man could have desired. Those miners who worked exclusively in "quartz diggings," were highly elated at the summer-like weather which this month brought, and those miners who worked in ravines, would have rejoiced had the rain descended nearly the whole time; but ultimately all were pleased, and each man worked with a will and energy worthy of the greatest success. During this month some of our citizens who had visited the "Eastern States," returned, accompanied by their wives and little ones, and these occasional arrivals of respectable ladies among us, exercised a marked improvement in the "manners and customs" of our heterogeneous population.

Whenever a former citizen arrived from the "East," he was at once surrounded by his acquaintances, and thoroughly questioned as to the events and occurrences that had transpired, and entreated for "a loan of the newspapers;" and speaking of newspapers, reminds me how eagerly they were read over, how thoroughly they were scanned with the hope of finding even a "a single paragraph" which might relate to this or that place, where the reader had lived or visited. The New York Herald and Tribune, New Orleans Delta and True Delta, were the papers most sought after; they retailed at from fifty cents to one dollar each, according to the supply. And who can wonder at the miners' being so interested about news from home? Were they not thousands of miles away? And does not every traveler, when far away from those he loved and esteemed, continually think and dream about his absent friends? and that constant thought of home, keeps the nervous system in continued feverish excitement and longing solicitude. I have often thought, whenever a person evinces a disposition to leave his home, or to tire of those who know and love him, that it would be well to send him off into some distant, half civilized community, and there, deprived of the comforts of home, and the companionship of long-tried and well known friends, it would cure him of a feverish, unsatisfied, and discontented disposition.

Until within a short time, the path to my "solitary abode on the mountain top," was clear and "well defined;" but now, as I have stated, that mode of mining resorted to by some, termed "kiotying," very materially interfered with my evening walks homeward. Often I was compelled to feel my way on "all fours," and being near-sighted, *I frequently jumped into a puddle of water supposing it to be a stone!* One dark and dreary night, when returning to my lone cabin, feeling my way, I made a leap, and alighted right in the —— water! Down, down I sank, until I was engulphed in liquid mud up to my arm-pits; fortunately I touched bottom, or I should have drowned, and no one near to lend a helping hand. Murder! murder!! murder!!! I cried lustily, but no answer. Again and again I called, help! help!! help!!! and still no answer, no help. Then I became unconscious. I had no fears; I was benumbed; the cold temperature of the foul liquid mud had chilled my entire system, and deadened all my faculties. Thus I remained until daylight, when an acquaintance, going out to procure fresh water, observed me, and with *awful yells*, called up the miners, who, in their kind efforts to *pull me out*, declared *that my bones cracked as though a pistol had been fired off!* I have elsewhere described that system of mining termed "kiotying," but it may not be inappropriate to say now, that even during daylight, after a hard rain, many persons refused to walk over the portion of ground thus worked.

A day or two subsequent to the unpleasant accident I have just related, Dr. —— was passing over nearly the same ground on his way to dinner. He anticipated no untoward accident; the ground seemed solid, and he could avoid the "dangerous passes." But look out! See there! A man has tumbled into a hole! Run men, run. There was the gallant doctor, more scared than hurt, almost hid from view, *embraced* by liquid mud. He was soon extricated, and like myself, did *not bless* those miners who burrowed under the ground at the risk of men's lives.

Sometimes fatal accidents occurred, which exemplified the old adage, that "in the midst of life we are in death." A miner was on his way to his cabin full of hope and joyful expectation, thinking of no accident, perhaps thinking of his absent family and the pleasure of soon meeting them; but, ah, how little all of us reflect upon the uncertainties of life! How little we think that in the "twinkling of an eye" we may be launched into eternity! Well, away he sped over the meadow and valley, until he reached his claim. He saluted his associates, and as their claim was worked some forty feet below the surface, it was necessary to descend in a bucket by means of a windlass; it was his turn to go down; he took his place in the bucket, and as he was being lowered, his innocent laugh seemed to re-echo around the deep cavern; he promised to send up "paying dirt," but crack, crack, snapped the rope—down he fell, and in a little while was brought up dead.

CHAPTER XXXIV.

CONSIDERABLE TALK ABOUT LEAVING CALIFORNIA—OUR POPULATION, &c., &c.

February and March, 1852. Well, I had at last decided upon returning home, and fixed upon the ensuing month of April for starting; and yet, kind friends urged me to stay; they told me of the thousands that were on their way hither; they told me of the impossibility of realizing one half the happiness I anticipated, in leaving California and returning to my kindred, and they urged me to "stay yet a little longer," and wait further developments; but my mind was made up, I had seen "the elephant" in all his phases; I had traversed the hills and valleys of Callifornia where previously white men had never ventured ; I had worked faithfully, often beyond my strength, and I had succeeded better than I had a right to expect, and I felt that I must seek the society of those whom I hoped still loved and remembered me ; but privately, I had not the same buoyant spirits as many others, for I had really no home on earth ; my parents had long since found rest and peace in heaven; but I still felt an uncontrollable desire to visit my native place, where I fondly believed some few were waiting patiently for my return. Therefore, my readers may soon expect a termination of "the incidents of a miner's life ;" but now in lieu thereof, I will take them on another voyage ; we will visit other countries, see strange sights and customs, and finally reach the great metropolis, New York.

The weather during February and March was delightful—in truth, the winter just ended, with the exception of a few days of rain and wind, was far more agreeable than the preceding summer. The facilities for mining were never more favorable, and miners lost no time in working out their claims ; still a large number of men, when night set in, donned their best attire, and frequented the cotillion parties, and succeeded so well in driving "dull care away," that a stranger could not have recognized in the well-dressed and oftentimes polished gentleman, the hardy, industrious, and rough-looking miner.

Our population embraced representatives from various quarters of the globe. We had the polite and volatile Frenchman, ready for "a trip on the light fantastic toe," or to cook you a dinner à la Soyer. The tall, haughty, and well proportioned John Bull, who never "saw anything to equal her most gracious Majesty's possessions on land and sea." The Emerald Isle also was well represented by delegates who could handle the pick and shovel as easily as they could assure you that they "niver saw a finer fellow in all their life than that mon there;" and we had the economical and industrious German, who delighted as much in his pipe and krout, seemingly, as he did in hoarding up his earnings; and the Jew, he was around offering clothing "at less price than you could buy the raw material," and last, and least respected, we had a numerous delegation from the "flowery kingdom," the weasel-eyed Chinamen. But I never disliked them as many others did; they never interfered in our national or municipal politics, and invariably minded their own business; which commendable characteristic some others might have imitated. They were clannish, because they were entirely unacquainted with our language and customs; but their desires were moderate; knowing the animosity at all times evinced towards them, they quietly took possession of discarded claims, or else took pre-emption right over ground, with which none other would have been content. I never knew a Chinaman to purchase any but black tea. "Me want black tea, green tea no good;" and when they purchased boots, something by the way, they hardly ever saw until they reached America, they always selected a pair twice the size of their feet; they appeared when walking to shove their feet along; their clothing was of the deepest indigo-blue color, and their bump of curiosity seemed largely developed, for they were always peeping around, gazing curiously at the doings and workings of American men and machinery.

At this period, dogs were a rarity, and commanded an exorbitant price. A German "just from Berlin," brought with him a fine specimen of the canine species, for which he was offered, but refused four hundred dollars. One day while he was sauntering through the woods adjacent to Centreville, his pet dog running by his side, some miscreant either intentionally or by accident, shot his only friend, his faithful dog, dead, and the poor man seemed as much distressed as though one of his immediate kindred had been killed.

I had disposed of my claims and implements, and devoted my time to fluting, doctoring, merchandizing, law quibbling, and speculating in rocks and sand, and my pecuniary receipts were greater than ever; and now that I had determined to leave California, the life I had led seemed almost enchanting, especially when listening to the sweet carols of the numerous beautiful little birds that built their nests in the trees, surrounding my cabin, and greeted me with their morning songs. But I began to wonder how such an one was doing, and who still lived to remember me, and who was laid in the silent grave. I contrasted my present feelings with those I experienced when I first landed in California; then all was doubt and uncertainty; then I missed the familiar faces of the friends I had left behind, and thought only of the pleasures of home. Now I felt mingled pain and pleasure, pain at parting from men and things that had become familiar to me, and pleasure at the delightful prospect of soon grasping by the hand, friends for whom I entertained undying attachment; in short, it all seemed as a dream, as though the earth was one grand theatre, and I enacting some subordinate part, and here closes my sketches of "life among the miners."

CHAPTER XXXV.

LEAVING THE MINES—BOUND FOR SACRAMENTO—INCIDENTS ALONG THE ROUTE, &c., &c.

The sun still lingered below the eastern horizon, the miners had not yet aroused from their slumbers, when, on the 25th of April, 1852, I stepped out of my humble cabin and looked around the valley where I had dwelt so many months—where I had worked, toiled, hoped and prayed. It was my last morning at the mines, my last look around a spot where I had enjoyed much pleasure, and had formed many agreeable acquaintances.

But at length the population gradually awoke from their slumbers, the lurid smoke from the numerous cabins began to ascend, and I gave a last look around the rude cabin that had sheltered me for many a night. I gazed again and again, and still once more, for the last time, upon the trees which I had planted, and with a sincere, heartfelt good bye, raised my bundle, turned away and left my California home forever!

I had engaged a seat in an uncovered wagon bound for Sacramento. Bidding a cordial farewell to friends standing around, I jumped to my seat beside the driver, who cracked his whip, and away we drove "over the hills and far away," and I could scarcely realize the fact that at last, after a long and tedious absence, after days of hoping and toiling, that I was on my way home. Aware of the inconvenience of much baggage, I carried only blankets, a change of linen, and my journal, and strange as it may appear, I experienced none of those happy feelings I had anticipated.

Our first stopping place was Rough and Ready, described in former pages. I was not aware of any necessity for our holding up here, unless to afford all hands an opportunity to take a swallow of the "ardent," smack their lips and light their pipes. Jehu seized the reins, sang out "git up!" and off we trotted.

I observed a passenger sitting quietly behind me, whose countenance indicated sobriety, manliness and respectability, although his garments were "all tattered and torn." Engaging in conversation, I learned his history. He had a month previously arrived here, had left a home, and a competency, for a ramble among the "highlands and lowlands" of California; and if in his wanderings he could secure a more comfortable dwelling-place than the home he left, he would settle down and send for his family; but ah! he had not thoroughly appreciated the comforts he once enjoyed; but he had since learned "to let well enough alone." He was on his way home, and expected that when his family would think it time to receive a letter from him, he would surprise them by presenting himself.

No particular incidents occurred during the morning to engage our attention. The sun was obscured by clouds, and occasionally a cold mist descended, which did not tend to enliven my sober feelings. We stopped at noon at the Zinc House for dinner, but soon again resumed our seats in the wagon. Towards the close of the day the sky became clear, the many beautiful flowers along the roadside seemed to smile upon us, saying, "come and gather us." Our driver whistled, sang and talked; he spurred on his horses, and we traveled along at a rapid pace; the reason was, "Jehu's" desire to reach the tavern a few miles ahead before the crowd came along. Now, the drivers along the route know the best inns, and the landlords always receive them kindly; for they find it to their interest to encourage the knights of the whip.

Our driver, with whom I became quite intimate, told me, "I'll take you to a tip-top house," and in due time we reached a house, which a sign swinging on high informed us was "Good's Kentucky House." Here we stopped, lodged and breakfasted. Our lodging room contained over a dozen cots, and some of them accommodated two lodgers. My bill was $2.25, quite reasonable, and when we took our seats in our "uncovered baggage wagon" early in the morning, we drove ahead with the delightful prospect of a clear, beautiful day. On our route, which was over the Sacramento plains, we feasted our eyes upon the largest, and most gorgeous flowers that we had so far come across. I would now and then trouble the driver to "hold his horses," and let the "wagon wait for me," until I had filled my pockets with the prettiest.

At noon we reached the "Star Hotel." Here we met a large number of Chinese on their way to the mines; patient, dull and good-natured fellows, all precisely alike in dress, manners and appearance. We dined at the "Star," price 75 cents; a capital dinner, clever landlord, and obliging waiters. After we were fed and rested, our captain, the driver, sang out, "get aboard," and away we went in fine style, until we came within sight of Sacramento.

The cost of my ride in the "slow but sure" line was six dollars. I was recommended by a friend in Grass Valley to stop at the "Lafayette House," and taking my bundle under my arm, I sought out the hotel, engaged board and lodging, and had no reason to regret my selection.

The boarders were generally an old-fashioned, sober set, who corresponded admirably with the "landlady and her sister-in-law;" but the appearance of the house and its entire furniture and accommodations were in striking contrast with the gorgeously embellished flash restaurants and hotels "around the corner." Our street, although but four or five years in existence, looked as though it had seen fifty summers come and go again. The reason was, that in the hurry to put up houses to accommodate the numerous impatient applicants, paint was left in the pot, instead of being applied to the buildings.

Tuesday, April 27.—I may have slept last night, but I cannot remember enjoying even a short nap. Fleas, musquitoes, and *et cetera*, appeared anxious to find out which could present me with the "most bills." Glad, indeed, was I when the glorious sun arose, and by its light enabled me to get up, walk out, and escape the numerous insects which had tormented me at night. Last evening the citizens held a large meeting in relation to the great influx of the "long tail" Chinamen; but I could not "feel" the necessity of driving them out of the country, when other foreigners are cordially invited and welcomed.

Understanding that the old, half-worn-out steamer Orient would pass Sacramento, I engaged passage for San Francisco; but, with several others I lounged about the wharf until midnight, and yet no Orient appeared; so I returned to the Lafayette, to wait until the regular steamer, the Antelope, sailed.

CHAPTER XXXVI.

SACRAMENTO CITY—DEPARTURE FOR SAN FRANCISCO—INCIDENT ON BOARD THE STEAMER—ARRIVAL AT THE METROPOLITAN CITY—ENGAGE PASSAGE FOR PANAMA—FIRE ON BOARD THE STEAMER, &c., &c.

Wednesday, April 28*th*, 1852.—Sacramento had wonderfully improved since I last passed through the city. Fine wide streets, profusely supplied stores, magnificent hotels and restaurants, and a levée which afforded protection from the inundations of the Sacramento river. I noticed lying on the wharf a large number of sturgeons and many other large sized fish, which were caught in the river, and produced considerable revenue to those persons engaged in following the profession of "Isaac Walton." Riding at anchor were a large number of vessels.

On shore a striking similitude to the wharves around New York city, was observable. What an enterprising, thorough-going people—how rapidly they have pushed on to wealth and luxury! But five years ago this bustling city, now teeming with life, was one vast plain—a wilderness.

I saw the hospitable Capt. Sutter; he whose lands first revealed the glittering metal that was secreted beneath the clods and rocks of California; and yet the discovery did not enrich him; his generous desire to benefit his fellow-men only resulted in his own loss; but I have since learned that the Legislature of California has made him ample restitution.

I lingered around the spacious and gaudily embellished saloons, and watched the eager crowds, observing that all—all, were bent upon acquiring money, money, money. Hark! the steamer has arrived, I hastened to the wharf, and saw at least five hundred Chinamen landing, on their way to the mines. Poor fellows, they were about to dwell in a land whose customs and manners were entirely dissimilar to those of their own flowery kingdom, and they knew they had to contend with the deep prejudice of the American settlers; they knew that they were disfranchised; but yet they had heard of the probability of accumulating money in a short time—in truth, fifty times faster than they could in their own country.

I settled my bill at the Lafayette House, and before long stood upon the forward deck of the steamer Antelope, awaiting the order of the Captain " to let go hauser, and 'bout ship." About 3 o'clock the " steam was let off," the wheels began to revolve, and we headed for the Bay of San Francisco.

I found several of my California acquaintances on board, and as the evening was damp and chilly, and the wind high, most of us sought the " between decks." I have never witnessed a more doleful and melancholy party—

and wherefore? Were we not going home? Had not our expectations been fulfilled? But ah! not until now did our true position press upon us; not until now, when we were " homeward bound," did we realize the length of time we had been absent, and begin to dread the changes that may have occurred during our absence. But away we steamed; now dodging a high bank, and then narrowly escaping running aground. On, on we sailed, until we arrived "safe and sound" at the wharf in San Francisco about 10 o'clock at night.

And here again what changes—what wonderful and almost incredible improvements had been successfully carried through, since my last visit. Carriages were in waiting to carry passengers to the different hotels; but taking my "blue bag" under my arm, and accompanied by my Ohio adventurer, I steered in a "bee line" for Smith's Temperance House. The room allotted to us was comfortably furnished, but the table was miserably supplied; however, unlike others I cared most for a clean and comfortable room.

Thursday, April 29*th*.—Chilly and disagreeable early in the morning, but, as usual in San Francisco, after 9 o'clock the temperature was delightful. During the morning I settled my bill at Smith's tavern, and took myself and "blue bag" to friend Welling's. Here I remained for several days. Friends again urged me to stay; W.

depicted, in glowing colors, the "certain prospect of ultimately coining money" but my mind was made up : I positively declared I would depart from San Francisco in the first comfortable steamer " up for Panama."

My leisure time was principally occupied in rambling around the city. What magnificent streets!—what substantial and commodious warehouses!—what elegant and comfortable mansions!—what conveniencies and opportunities for enjoying life : fine churches, respectable congregations—I could hardly believe that I was in California, where, a few short years previously, all was wild and desolate, naught but one vast wilderness.

On Tuesday, May 4, I called at the agent's office, and secured a ticket for "passage to Panama in the A No. 1, entirely new and substantially built, side-wheel steamer, Winfield Scott." She was not expected to start for a day or two, in consequence of an unusually large number of persons " bound for home."

The steamer was entirely new, staunch, and built expressly for the "California trade." I never saw space so admirably fitted up for carrying passengers ; even down to the lowest plank in the " hold," berths were fitted up. So we had accommodations for No. 1 passengers, second rate passengers, third rate passengers, fourth and fifth rate passengers ; but who cared for accommodations now? all we wanted was a speedy passage home.

Hark! Fire, fire, fire! " Hurry up, men, it's down on the wharf." I ran too, and soon discovered that the " A No. 1 entirely new and elegantly fitted up steamer Winfield Scott" was on fire. " Disappointed this time ; guess we'll have to remain in California after all." " Seize hold there!" " Lay too, Monumental." " Down with your hose!" " Now, now let fly ;" phiz, phiz; " she throws well." " Lift her lads, the vessel will be destroyed." "Hurrah! boys, we will save her yet," cries another. And sure enough, the gallant firemen subdued the flames ; the fire was soon extinguished, and in almost the time occupied in describing the incident, carpenters were at work repairing damages and thus prompt, active and energetic are the people of California.

CHAPTER XXXVII.

DEPARTURE FROM CALIFORNIA—LIFE ON BOARD A STEAMER—ARRIVAL AT ACAPULCO, MEXICO, &c., &c.

Thursday, May 6th, 1852.—An unusual commotion on the always crowded " Central Wharf" this morning. Drays, carriages, go-carts, and every other kind of carts were in motion along the wharf; people were hurrying forward, and had the question been asked, as doubtless it was, " What's going on down at the ' Central ? ' " the answer would have been, " the new steamer Winfield Scott, is about to start for Panama." Friend Welling accompanied me to the boat; we "talked our last talk," and were hurriedly partaking of breakfast at a stand near by, when the bell sounded. I hastily bade him a last good-bye, jumped aboard the steamer, and stood among over six hundred men, bound *not for California*, but for home!

What singular feelings came over me!—what hundreds of strange thoughts and sad memories crossed my brain. I could have laughed and wept at the same time; but see! the wheels begin to move, we are receding from the wharf, and cheer upon cheer is given for the Scott's passengers. Hats were twirled around, handkerchiefs were flung to the breeze; good-bye, good-bye and good-bye was given and returned. The "steam is up," and away we sailed, until I could just discern the crowd upon the wharf. By and by we passed the "Golden Gate," the entrance to the magnificent harbor of San Francisco, and soon lost sight of the land of gold; and now that *agreeable* epidemic, sea-sickness, began to appear among us. Some how or other I was "as fresh as a lark," and passed among the *awfully* sick passengers, telling them to look up, and in a day or two they would recover. Some declared they did not care "whether the vessel ran aground, sank, or blew up, they felt so sick."

Our vessel carried at least two hundred passengers more than she could comfortably accommodate, and the decks were so crowded, that a man really had not a place *to spit.* A sad state of affairs for an American! Some of our passengers were in high glee, and cherished the fondest, highest hopes ; others again were happy, but made no outward demonstrations, and others were sullen, thoroughly disappointed, and a few were stretched upon the decks, lost to all sense of hope or fear, and only wishing for grim death to remove them from this miserable world. Ding, ding, ling, dong, ling ; " all those steerage passengers who have not secured berths will call at the Purser's office, and secure the same," and they did not require a second bidding ; for the Purser's office was immediately crowded with " those steerage passengers who had not secured berths." The vessel was expressly built for the California trade, and even the smallest space was adapted to some use ; down, "way down in the hold " forward, several feet below the surface of the water, where usually in other vessels the ropes, chains, ship's rigging, &c., are stored, berths were fitted up from floor to ceiling, and hardly room enough left for a passenger to pass along. The place was dark ; daylight rarely penetrated there ; but at least fifty men occupied this apartment, for which the charge was seventy-five dollars each. Then there were steerage passengers, who paid one hundred dollars each, who were allowed the second deck to sleep in—much more comfortable than the "hold" below, and where they enjoyed a little more daylight, and above these, on the third deck, were still higher-paying passengers, who had comfortable berths and bedding, and then we reach another class, who sleep on this deck, but eat in the cabin, "after the third table." Then still another class, by paying fifty dollars more, sleep on "standee berths aft," having the privilege of the "quarter deck," and can promenade "abaft the wheel house," but are required to eat at table No. 2; that is, after first cabin passengers have eaten, and last, but the first class on board, were the first cabin passengers, first table, choice of state-rooms, and the privileges and hospitalities of the whole vessel. This class, (and, by the way, every one who can afford it, should always take a first cabin ticket,) had to pay over a hundred dollars more than anybody else on board.

Our passengers were as various in their phrenological and physiognomical developments as possibly could be. We had the proud and peacock passenger, the clever, substantial and successful passenger, the kind-hearted and considerate passenger, the guerilla-looking passenger, the envious passenger, the fault-finding and dissatisfied passenger, and the sneaking, hang-dog-looking passenger, and so on—so on. Most of the passengers slept during the voyage, on the upper deck, for the temperature was hot and exceedingly oppressive, and it could not be otherwise; for we were "directly under the sun," and near the "equatorial line." I suffered more on board this steamer than upon any vessel on which I had traveled, owing to the crowd, extremely hot weather, and the utter impossibility of procuring one night's refreshing sleep.

On Friday morning, May, 14th, we made the harbor of Acapulco, Mexico. The steamer Golden Gate was just sailing away from it, bound for San Francisco, and was more densly crowded than our vessel. I afterwards learned that she had fifteen hundred passengers on board; but men were bound for California, they never stopped to inquire about accommodations.

On Saturday I went ashore, and easily recognized the place, (described in a former chapter,) and to any one visiting a Mexican town in 1852, I will warrant—that if no fire, earthquake or inundation destroys it, he will recognize the place twenty years thereafter. I pronounce the Mexicans unhesitatingly, the most dull, thriftless and unconcerned set of mortals I have ever encountered; at least, such as I met. I ordered breakfast at a café, which was little better prepared to accommodate guests than an Esquimaux would be at his inhospitable home.

A large number of vessels make this place their rendezvous, and all the California steamers anchor here for the purpose of coaling, watering and provisioning; and as most of the passengers go ashore, what a fine harvest enterprising people could reap; but the lazy natives just stand and lounge about, gazing at the enterprising strangers coming and going, and manifest very little, if any concern, about anything outside their own squalid homes.

CHAPTER XXXVIII.
DEPARTURE FROM ACAPULCO—SCENES ON BOARD THE STEAMER—ARRIVAL AT PANAMA—INCIDENTS BY THE WAY-SIDE, &c., &c.

Saturday, May 15th, 1852.—Feeling somewhat wearied by my rambles through the insignificant town of Acapulco, I was about to rest myself beneath the wide-spreading branches of a tree, which stood on an eminence, commanding a fine view of the town and harbor, when, boom ! sounded from the cannon on board the steamer, that put a *quietus* to all contemplation of Mexican scenery or anything else, but a desire to get aboard a little more expeditiously than I came ashore. Looking up and down the street, the Scott's passengers were seen hurrying to the landing, and such a scrambling into the " dug-outs," canoes and old whale boats, is only seen when a steamer gives her last signal to her truant passengers to wake up and come aboard. About 4 o'clock we hoisted anchor and " headed " for Panama; the temperature was about as comfortable as a baker's oven thoroughly heated, and if there were any pleasant looking passengers on board I did not see them. On a platform, " forward the wheelhouse," on either side of the vessel, the " live stock," consisting of steers, sheep, and pigs, were penned, and every day or two the butcher of the vessel slaughtered some of them to furnish the cabin table with fresh meat. The steerage passengers enjoyed the privilege of " looking at the cattle confined in the pen." On the " larboard side " of the steamer, near the "foremast," was a " little crib," which attracted more visitors than any other part of the vessel, it being the place for retailing the " ardent; " twenty-five cents would procure a glass of brandy, *plain ;* thirty-eight cents *brandy with ice.* I was often amused at the frequent calls for brandy *straight*, by passengers who were *seriously indisposed.* I was informed our population numbered nine hundred, and it was remarkable that no one died, for as I mentioned in a former chapter, some were lying on the deck who looked more dead than alive; their constitutions completely broken down by sickness and exposure at the mines. The cook on board a vessel is a perfect autocrat; those passengers who are " ticketed for the steerage " submit to any amount of insolence, merely to procure some extra food or the privileges of the galley, and as the cooks are nearly all representatives from Africa, they exercise more authority than the Emeperor of Hayti.

Our Captain, or skipper, as he was sometimes called,

appeared to be a sturdy, resolute chap, and like all steamer "executive officers," knew how to enjoy himself, and strut the "quarter deck," master of all he surveyed. The chief engineer was provided with a snug little office in which to make his calculations. The first mate was a tall resolute chap, but appeared to have fifty per cent. less to do than mate No. 2, who was a small, tough, and exceedingly obedient officer. The firemen, coal men, ash men, &c., whose duties confined them in a hold, so dark that daylight never penetrated, had "windsails" erected to supply them with fresh air, and thus their lives were preserved; nevertheless, they were occasionally brought on deck to revive them, for the heat "below" was intense. The sailors were pretty much like the general run of "forecastle" men, not appearing to care much for themselves or anybody else.

On Saturday, May 22d, we reached the anchorage about ten miles, *more or less*, from Panama. Now all was excitement and confusion ; the passengers forgot all concern about cabin or steerage accommodations. The question was how to reach Panama, and when?— The day was fast declining ; a thick mist was lowering upon us, but we could perceive small boats making for the ship. At length the boats of various size and design reached us, and the natives cried out—"go ashore," "go ashore;" "me take you 'shore for two dollars"—"hah! signor, take my boat, me go quick!—but Uncle Samuel's mails had first right, then the lady passengers came next, and finally the privilege was extended to all the passengers to "vamose in double quick time." Presenting to my Ohio adventurer my blankets, and reserving only a change of linen for myself, I climbed down the side of the vessel and alighted in an old mud scow, just in time to secure a delightful sail to the ancient city of Panama. There were about a dozen of us on board, all strangers to each other; but we soon formed a community of social and friendly travelers; our old scow seemed to have been distanced by the other boats; our boatmen looked as though they could murder and pitch us overboard as easily as they poured forth their horrid oaths; and it was not until dark night overshadowed us, that we reached the outside of the remains of a dilapidated wall, which I believe once encompassed the city; but our troubles were not yet ended; the boatmen demanded extra compensation to carry us through the mud, at the same time ordering us out of the boat in true Spanish fashion, to the infinite amusement of the hang-dog looking crowd of natives who were standing around watching a chance to pilfer; the mud was at least two feet deep to the landing, a distance of about two yards, and things looked squally; but seeing a big fellow about to wade through for the purpose of fastening the boat rope to a post, I leaped upon his back and compelled him to cary me ashore "*nolens volens.*" I stood upon a rock waiting for the rest of the passengers, and after a while they all landed, and we pushed ahead hardly knowing whether we were going " up or down hill," or in the right or wrong direction ; the street was dark, muddy, and narrow ; we were followed by the natives, who kept up a chattering around us like so many monkeys, until at last we reached the centre of the city, where we found a "numerous delegation" of " *Los Yankee;* " and when I heard my name called, I turned, and was agreeably surprised to find some of my acquaintances from California, who at once introduced me to the landlord of the "American House," who accommodated me with a room in which only fifty men were to to sleep ! After partaking of a supper fit only for an aboriginal to enjoy, I ventured forth to " see the sights," but as the night was dark, and the authorities not approving of lighting the streets, I retraced my steps, and feeling jaded and wearied, I sought rest on my cot.

CHAPTER XXXIX.

PANAMA.—A NIGHT'S LODGING—A PEDESTRIAN EXPEDITION TO GORGONA, Etc, Etc.

Saturday, May 22, 1852.—We frequently hear persons say, "I did not sleep a wink last night," but if the truth were known, they had slept half the time; and I was about to say the same of the night of the 21st, but I believe I did doze, although I grumbled as much as any other lodger. There were about fifty men lodged in one room. We slept on cots, or rather reclined on cots, hardly two of which were alike.

"Slap, flap, bang"—"confound these musquitoes;" "slap, slap, bang," "what's that?" "See there, what big roaches, lizards, and centipedes!" "Look out, fellows, they'll tumble down on you before you know it." "Bang, slap, bang; pshaw, I'll get up, dress, and go down stairs." "Pooh, who would live in such a wretched country?" "Who can sleep in such an insect-infested hole as this?" And in truth, forbearance ceased to be a virtue. I tried the expedient of covering myself with bed clothes; that would n't answer, for I came near being melted. I threw off the sheets; an army of insects attacked me "fore and aft." However, daylight at length condescended to peer through the dirty, prison-looking windows, and such a tumbling down stairs was only familiar to the quercitron-dyed landlord, who flourished at the American.

It was the rainy season on the isthmus, and were I not homeward-bound, I might have felt most uncomfortable. My bill for supper, lodging and breakfast was only one dollar and fifty cents. I strolled around the city, and noticed that in the business portion of the town the houses were three-storied, "*originally*" white-washed, balconies running along the second story which had been painted red about ninety years ago—more or less. The streets were very narrow, filth abundant, and the markets remarkable only, for a want of order and cleanliness; meat and vegetables inviting to a stranger.

The loquacious parrot and the nimble and thieving monkey appeared to be the happiest *citizens*. The signoritas were attired in loose and flowing robes that admirably suited the warm climate, and I was so favorably impressed with the attractions of the ancient city of Panama, that I determined to leave for Gorgona on foot and alone, despite the heavy shower that was beating down.

I had not proceeded far out of the city ere I began to wish that the others would follow. I stopped at a mud hut, drank coffee, and by the time I was ready to depart, there came along a crowd of Americans, each one, like myself, traveling on "shanks' mare," and a merry party we were; away we went, now tumbling into mud deeper than we desired, and again picking over way over solid rock by a rugged path wide enough for a mule to pass. But "look there!" "what is that?" It was a poor mule that had sunk in the mud, and been left by its owner to die. We strove to pull him out, but we failed, and so left him to his fate.

The rain poured down furiously, but on we traveled; and anon the clouds would break away and the glorious sun shine forth, even here. About every five miles we came across thatched huts, in which brandy and coffee was dispensed at ten cents a swallow, and the natives seemed to be well encouraged, for the wayworn travelers needed refreshments. We continued our slow and wearisome march up hill and down hill, through mud and over rough stones, until we reached the "Half-way Settlement," where we concluded to hold up until the following morning.

The house, or rather the tent, at which we stopped was conducted by an American woman, who was as gentle and kind-hearted as an enraged tigress. Her face must have contained 90 per cent. of brass, and her heart have been composed of stone. Here we were privileged to "pile ourselves" on top of a load of wood, and if any of the party were comfortable that night, I never heard of it.

Sunday, May 23.—I should not have known it was the Sabbath day only for the regular posting in my journal. We ate breakfast—and such a breakfast!—settled bills, and left the inhospitable "Half-way House" with no friendly feelings to our hostess or her miserable shanty.

Away we trudged for Gorgona; the pathway was hemmed in by low chapparral, a fit hiding place for the numerous serpents said to abound there, but who *politely* kept out of our way. I observed a large quantity of the sensitive plant growing luxuriantly around, but I did not see "those lovely flowers" I had been told we would find in our travels; but we overtook myriads of large black ants who kept on their course, regardless of everything but themselves.

Towards the close of the day we espied Gorgona, and the first hut we reached I entered, ordered supper, and sat down to rest myself with all the importance of a steamboat captain. My hotel had no floor, no beds, not a table, and I was curious to know how my host would arrange matters. After considerable delay, he brought in an old box, covered it with *unbleached* muslin, and then placed my meal on it, which consisted of fried bananas, eggs, and a bottle of claret wine. I enjoyed the repast, (charge, sixty cents,) and soon after sallied forth in quest of novelty, and was surprised to find "further down the road" quite a settlement, several hotels conducted by enterprising Americans, the principal houses being the Union and the St. Louis, and at the end of the lane I discovered the Chagres river, not near so formidable a stream as I had been led to expect. Finding most of the Americans quartered at the Union and St. Louis hotels, I concluded to retrace my steps, procure my bundle, and board at the Union.

I noticed a number of signoritas dressed in white going in and coming out of a hut; curiosity led me thither, and I saw the body of a child lying in state; the friends were showering flowers over the little one, but it appeared that a death at Gorgona was regarded more as a cause for rejoicing than weeping. I reached my "suburban retreat," and in as good Spanish and English as I could command, gave my half-clad host to understand that "I would vamose down the lane where Los Americano crowded." After many bows and *warm* expressions of regard, we separated, and I was in a short time standing on the balcony of the Union hotel watching the vast crowd of homeward-bound travelers gathered around, not two of whom were dressed alike, and each sadly needing the barber.

Understanding that the cots were nearly all taken, I made application to the landlord, who secured me one just in time, or I should have been compelled to sleep on the damp floor, as a goodly number did.

The sky was overcast, and the temperature moist and chilly. I would have preferred a seat in the kitchen to dry my clothing, but there was no alternative. I had to lounge about the only spare place, the bar-room, which was damp, overcrowded, and *not* perfumed with either the rose or jessamine.

CHAPTER XL.

A SAIL DOWN THE CHAGRES RIVER—SCENES AT TIVOLI—THE RAILROAD—DEPARTURE FOR, AND ARRIVAL AT, ASPINWALL.

Monday, May 24, 1852.—Overcome by fatigue, I slept well last night; arose early this morning, partook of a tolerable breakfast, and then paid $2.80 for supper, lodging and breakfast to the landlord of "Union hotel," Gorgona.

Now commenced another unpleasant task, to select out of the many "dug-outs," one to convey my honorable body down the river to a place called Tivoli. After bargaining some time with the half-clad natives, I at length selected one in which I found several Americans, among them my Ohio acquaintance. Our fare was four dollars each; distance not over twenty miles. A "dug-out" is a boat manufactured from the thickest part of a tree, and so unsafe to sail in, that if a passenger should chance to lean over on one side, it would upset, and then, according to some journalists, look out for alligators.

Taking a last, and I hope eternal farewell of Gorgona,

our boatmen sang out, "all ready," and off we sailed about as fast as the current was pleased to take us, no thanks to the copper-colored boatmen. We had not proceeded very far, and had hardly become familiar with our unsymmetrical "dug-out," when the "gentleman from Ohio" fell forward in my lap, very nearly upsetting our rickety old craft. The frequent indulgence in "Darien fruits" put him "*hors du combat*," to the serious annoyance of our native boatmen, who cared as much for the sick man as they did for a log of wood. We could not administer any relief, and were compelled to let him groan and suffer, only wishing that we had some medicine or cordial to give him.

About noon we reached the *great city* of Tivoli, and I had the sick man placed in "Old Joe's" hotel, where he was as comfortably provided for as circumstances would permit. I found Tivoli the dirtiest, meanest, most contemptible fever and ague breeding hole it ever fell to my lot to visit. There were about a dozen thatched huts, with accommodations a shade better than a decent pigpen.

As soon as possible I purchased a ticket for Aspinwall, distant eighteen miles, fare, five dollars; but unfortunately we received intelligence that some accident had happened, and we should be compelled to wait here until the succeeding day.

Hundreds of homeward-bound Americans were quartered

here awaiting the arrival of the cars, consequently they "ate and drank" everything the shiftless natives could muster. This place was the first way station and terminus, at that time, of the Panama railroad. Many of the natives were unfriendly to the road, because it deprived them of a fine revenue from boating, etc., but now the road is completed to Panama, and the journey attended with more pleasure than discomfort.

In my walks around, I chanced to enter a dirty-looking shanty, and make the acquaintance of the proprietor. He was a young man from "down east," who had ventured out here for the purpose of "bettering his finances." The unhealthy climate, the miasmatic effluvia arising from the damp and filthy village and its surroundings, had seriously impaired his health; he looked to be more dead than alive. I suggested the propriety of leaving this death-inviting place; but he replied, "I have a fine chance to accumulate money here, and if I go away, what can I do? I came here to make money, and I am bound to see it through." I hope he was successful and escaped death; but it certainly was a miserable hole for a white man to dwell in.

The Ohio traveler soon recovered his usual health, and agreed with me, that his illness was occasioned by indulging too freely in tropical fruits.

While I discountenanced the habitual use of brandy, still, in journeying through such places as Panama, Gorgona, and Tivoli, it were better to use brandy moderately than to indulge in the tempting tropical fruits.

Tuesday, May 25.—There were no sleeping accommodations for the passengers; some slept on the railroad track, because it was cleaner than the village; others secured seats in the cars, and I walked, talked, and occasionally nodded during the night, which seemed almost interminable; but as everything has an end, our unpleasant night at Tivoli came to one, and daylight broke and shed abroad its cheering light on the wearied and restless travelers.

"Hark! what's that?" "Three cheers, men, the cars are coming!" and true, here comes dashing along the train —the cars crowded with men, women and children, bound for California. As the steam-horse stopped his snorting, a shower of rain suddenly descended, scattering the travelers in all directions in search of shelter, for when it rains on the Isthmus "it rains hogsheads of water in a solid stream." After awhile the shower ceased, the clouds passed away, and the sun deigned to shine upon Tivoli. The numerous ladies on the train had my fullest sympathy for the "hard road they had to travel," and my sincere wishes for the realization of their expectations.

As soon as the California gold-seekers were out of the cars, we homeward-bound travelers rushed to the seats, and it is unnecessary to say, anxiously waited for the train to move off. The cars were built in the United States expressly for the climate of Darien, were cheerful in appearance and very comfortable. Soon the conductor sang out, "all aboard," and away we went in gallant style for Aspinwall. The road was in excellent condition, so far as I was able to judge. The thick, luxuriant shrubbery which lined the road on either side precluded an opportunity of " seeing the country."

About mid-day we arrived at Aspinwall, being the only place this side of California which bore any resemblance to the "land of the free and the home of the brave." The railroad company had erected a long, well-covered shed, extending a considerable distance out into the bay, which allowed steamers to anchor alongside, to the great convenience and gratification of travelers.

CHAPTER XLI.

ASPINWALL—AFLOAT AGAIN—BOUND FOR NEW YORK—INCIDENTS ON BOARD THE STEAMER—STATEN ISLAND—ARRIVAL AT NEW YORK—THE END.

Upon our arrival at Aspinwall, we found several steamers "up for the States," which occasioned *intense* gratification to the large number of "homeward-bound" passengers just emerging from the cars and busily engaged in hunting up their baggage. As I had no baggage to trouble me, I hastened at once to the first steamer lying most conveniently to the railroad wharf—sought out the purser's office, and purchased a cabin ticket for New York for twenty-five dollars. I was most *agreeably* disappointed in finding the fare so much reduced; the usual rate had been from eighty to one hundred dollars for cabin fare : but the unusual number of opposition steamers meeting there at the same time caused the reduction.

My apparel was so coarse and well-worn ; my spectacles about five times heavier than they should have been, and my whiskers and moustache so rough and *irregular*, that I really felt ashamed to show myself in the saloon of the steamer. Nevertheless, passengers from California were always treated with respect, because they were supposed to carry the "needful" about them.

On the wharf, the first sight that reminded me of my return to civilized communities, was that of observing Irishmen selling apples and cakes! Aspinwall appears to have been built in the midst of a swamp, whose rank and luxuriant grass and weeds afford admirable resting places for those affectionate little bill stickers, musquitoes, to say nothing of insects and reptiles of whose habits and peculiarities I had rather read, than observe for myself!

The steamer on which I had engaged passage proved to be the Crescent City, which subsequently became better known for the animosity the Habaneros entertained for her and her purser.

About 4 o'clock, P. M., we let go the "fastenings," and steamed away for the great city of New York. My feelings were more delightful than I care to express. The accommodations on board the "Crescent" were comfortable and elegant. We had few passengers, and for the first time in four years, I was traveling comfortably, and felt as happy as a school-boy returning to his home.

Happening to be seated in the main saloon when supper was announced, I took my seat at the table with several agreeable acquaintances. The steward handed me a ticket, on which was printed—"First cabin, first table, first state-room." This was very fortunate for me, for those passengers that still remained on deck were required to eat at the second table, and when they "came below" and found how the tickets were distributed, they were not the happiest passengers on board. We had the Minister Plenipotentiary and suite of Peru on their way to Rome; several ladies from other portions of South America; a Lieutenant of the United States Navy returning from a distant clime on the "sick list;" several English families on their way home, after a prolonged absence in Chili; and the remainder Californians, with heavy moustaches and bushy beards,—some wearing blue, red, calico, and hickory shirts, and boots so well nailed, that carpets were perforated like a sand-box. One chap wore in his old blue blanket shirt bosom, a fine specimen of gold, worth at least two hundred dollars; another wore blue overalls, a blue shirt, and I was about to say—a blue face, but he had ten thousand dollars in his possession, and if the feelings of his heart had been unfolded, a happier person could not have been discovered on board.

As I remarked before, my apparel was of *such fine texture*, that I declined state-room accommodations, and willingly surrendered them for a "standee berth." I cannot recollect ever having been on a vessel where I observed less "noise and confusion;" every man appeared to know his place, and everything had its place. The table was most beautifully and luxuriantly furnished, and the returning Californians did ample justice to the viands.

Among the passengers was a little Spanish girl, about six years of age, who became very much attached to me. Her father had died but a short time before, and her mother was pursuing her journey without an escort: This little child would watch for my appearance early in the morning, and continue with me until evening, and yet not one word of English could she speak. But I thought the little one felt sad and lonely; or, perhaps, I may have resembled her father. At all events, she was my most frequent companion during the voyage; although with her mother I never exchanged a word or salutation. The passengers remarked how happy the little one appeared in my society; but the voyage over, I lost sight of her forever. If still living, she may possibly remember the care and attention I paid her when a little child journeying away from her home and native land, and traveling among a people with whose language and customs she was wholly unacquainted.

The waiters generally on board vessels returning with California passengers, are very attentive and obedient— cheered by the hope of receiving a "large fee" at the end of the voyage. The waiter for our mess was kept continually on the march.

During our residence in California we had been deprived of many comforts and delicacies; so all now appeared disposed to secure a large share of the good things placed

before us day after day. The gentleman who sat nearest
me was an admirable " compagnon de voyage ; " he would
direct " John " to bring him first this, and then that dish,
and it always seemed that he ordered precisely *what I
wished;* so he had the trouble of ordering, and I, the pleasure of partaking.

On Friday, June 4, we came within sight of Staten
Island. The weather was hazy and damp; but the
foreigners especially, crowded the upper decks to catch a
glimpse of Yankee land. John Bull was in ecstasies;
"beautiful," "charming." he would would exclaim. Signor
Spaniola looked on in silence. But hark! the bell rings,
the wheels cease their revolutions—we are off the quarantine station. The health officer boarded us ; all right—
we were too much excited to be on the sick list. We
steamed up ; boom ! our little cannon fired off—the sound
reverberates and re-echoes along the shore. " Wake up,
men," a California steamer is coming up ; away we go—
now nearing the forests of masts along the wharves ; now
we perceive the city—what a collection of stone and mortar! see, there is Williamsburgh, and there Brooklyn;
still we go on—round the Battery ; now we move slowly,
"look out there!" "catch that rope," "make fast;"
" stand back, gentlemen "—" the United States mails take
precedence," " clear the gangway." Out come the mails,
and up come the hotel runners—*kind gentlemen;*—" yes,
11*

sir;" "Astor House"—"French's Hotel"—"Irving House"—"take your baggage, sir"—"first rate home; all the Californians stop there." "Whew! all is confusion;"—"get off there"—"don't crowd so;" "knock that fellow down." But I rolled my blue bag under my arm, marched forward, and left the vessel?

The voyage was over! My spirits were weighed down with an uncontrollable melancholy; I almost wished I had remained in California, or was landing in San Francisco instead of New York; nor was I singular in this respect; most travelers who have been away from home for a long time, after years of toil and excitement, and then at length return, the transition is so sudden, the change so great, that they cannot at once realize the fact.

I was desirous of reaching the hotel by a different route from that usually taken, to conceal from the loafing crowd around that I was a returned Californian. I succeeded admirably. I stopped at Johnston & Roger's hotel, in Fulton street, where I had boarded for some time prior to my journey to California. The hotel presented the same appearance; the attachés were the same, excepting only the clerk in the office, as when I left in 1849. It seemed as but yesterday; I could hardly believe I had been absent so long. As soon as I reached the room assigned me, I took out my old razor—

quickly removed my moustache and whiskers—sallied out to the nearest clothing store, purchased a new suit of clothes—took a capital bath, and then sat down in the reading room of the hotel as unconcerned as though I had not a few hours previously left the steamer, and just concluded a three years' residence in the wilds of California.

THE END.

www.ingramcontent.com/pod-product-compliance
Lightning Source LLC
Chambersburg PA
CBHW020806230426
43666CB00007B/885